OFFICIATING BASEBALL

A publication for the National Federation of State High School
Associations Officials Education Program

Developed by the
American Sport Education Program

Human Kinetics

Library of Congress Cataloging-in-Publication Data

Officiating Baseball : American Sport Education Program with National Federation of State High School Associations.

    p. cm.

Includes index.

ISBN 0-7360-4770-0 (soft cover)

1. Baseball--Umpiring. 2. Sports officiating. I. National Federation of State High School Associations.

GV876.O44 2004

796.357'3--dc22

                 2003027578

ISBN: 0-7360-4770-0

The Web addresses cited in this text were current as of November 2003, unless otherwise noted.

NFHS Officials Education Program Coordinator: Mary Struckhoff; **Project Consultant:** Elliot Hopkins, CAA, NFHS Baseball Rules Editor; **Project Writer:** Thomas Hanlon; **Acquisitions Editors:** Renee Thomas Pyrtel and Greg George; **Developmental Editor:** Laura Pulliam; **Assistant Editors:** Scott Hawkins, Kim Thoren, and Mandy Maiden; **Copyeditor:** Bob Replinger; **Proofreader:** Alisha Jeddeloh; **Indexers:** Robert and Cynthia Swanson; **Graphic Designer:** Andrew Tietz; **Graphic Artist:** Tara Welsch; **Photo Manager:** Dan Wendt; **Cover Designer:** Jack W. Davis; **Photographer (cover):** © Human Kinetics; **Photographer (interior):** Dan Wendt; photos on pages 1, 5, 9, 15, 19, 125, 129, 132, 137, 138, 142, 146, and 151 © Human Kinetics; **Art Manager:** Kareema McLendon; **Illustrator:** Keith Blomberg and Mic Greenberg; **Printer:** United Graphics

We thank the High School of Saint Thomas More in Champaign, Illinois, for assistance in providing the location for the photo shoot for this book.

Printed in the United States of America   10 9 8 7 6 5 4 3 2 1

Human Kinetics

Web site: www.HumanKinetics.com

United States: Human Kinetics
P.O. Box 5076, Champaign, IL 61825-5076
800-747-4457
e-mail: humank@hkusa.com

Canada: Human Kinetics
475 Devonshire Road Unit 100
Windsor, ON N8Y 2L5
800-465-7301 (in Canada only)
e-mail: orders@hkcanada.com

Europe: Human Kinetics
107 Bradford Road, Stanningley
Leeds LS28 6AT, United Kingdom
+44 (0) 113 255 5665
e-mail: hk@hkeurope.com

Australia: Human Kinetics
57A Price Avenue, Lower Mitcham
South Australia 5062
08 8277 1555
e-mail: liaw@hkaustralia.com

New Zealand: Human Kinetics
Division of Sports Distributors NZ Ltd.
P.O. Box 300 226 Albany
North Shore City, Auckland
0064 9 448 1207
e-mail: blairc@hknewz.com

CONTENTS

PREFACE

It's no secret that umpires are an essential part of America's favorite pastime. But how do baseball umpires come to know their stuff? How do they keep all the rules and mechanics straight throughout every game and every season? Educational tools and reference materials—such as this book—are useful in helping officials not only learn their craft but also stay sharp. *Officiating Baseball* is a key resource for those who want to umpire baseball games at the high school level. The mechanics you'll find here are developed by the National Federation of State High School Associations (NFHS) and used for high school baseball throughout the United States.

We expect that you know at least a little about baseball but perhaps not much about officiating it. Or you might know lots about both. In any case, the overall objective of *Officiating Baseball* is to prepare you to officiate games, no matter what your level of experience. More specifically, this book will

- introduce you to the culture of officiating baseball,
- tell you what will be expected of you as a baseball umpire,
- explain and illustrate the mechanics of officiating baseball in detail,
- show a connection between the rules of baseball and the mechanics of officiating it, and
- serve as a reference for you throughout your officiating career.

Officiating Baseball covers baseball officiating basics, baseball officiating mechanics and specific play situations. In part I you'll read about who baseball umpires are and what qualities you'll find in a good baseball umpire. Part I also differentiates high school officiating from officiating at youth and college levels and completely describes game responsibilities, including pregame and postgame duties. Part II, the meat of the book, describes plate and field umpire mechanics and two-, three- and four-umpire systems, all in careful detail. You'll find these mechanics chapters well organized and amply illustrated. Part III highlights some key cases from the *NFHS Baseball Case Book* and shows how you, the umpire, apply the rules in action.

Officiating Baseball is a practical how-to guide that is approved by the NFHS. This book is also the text for the *NFHS Officiating Baseball Methods* online course, which also has been developed and produced by the American Sport Education Program (ASEP) as part of the NFHS Officials Education Program. To find out how you can register for the online course, visit www.ASEP.com.

NFHS OFFICIALS CODE OF ETHICS

Officials at an interscholastic athletic event are participants in the educational development of high school students. As such, they must exercise a high level of self-discipline, independence and responsibility. The purpose of this code is to establish guidelines for ethical standards of conduct for all interscholastic officials.

- Officials shall master both the rules of the game and the mechanics necessary to enforce the rules, and shall exercise authority in an impartial, firm and controlled manner.
- Officials shall work with each other and their state associations in a constructive and cooperative manner.
- Officials shall uphold the honor and dignity of the profession in all interaction with student-athletes, coaches, athletic directors, school administrators, colleagues and the public.
- Officials shall prepare themselves both physically and mentally, shall dress neatly and appropriately and shall comport themselves in a manner consistent with the high standards of the profession.
- Officials shall be punctual and professional in the fulfillment of all contractual obligations.
- Officials shall remain mindful that their conduct influences the respect that student-athletes, coaches and the public hold for the profession.
- Officials shall, while enforcing the rules of play, remain aware of the inherent risk of injury that competition poses to student-athletes. When appropriate, they shall inform event management of conditions or situations that appear unreasonably hazardous.
- Officials shall take reasonable steps to educate themselves about recognizing emergency conditions that might arise during the competition.

KEY TO DIAGRAMS

 Umpire starting position

 Umpire ending position

 Player

• • • Batted ball

- - - Umpire path

- – – Throw

PART I

BASEBALL OFFICIATING
BASICS

CHAPTER 1

INTRODUCTION TO BASEBALL OFFICIATING

You probably became an umpire because you love the sport of baseball. You most likely played baseball at some level and want to remain connected to the sport.

You're hardly alone. Baseball is one of America's most popular and most enduring sports. (The first game was played in 1846, and today approximately 455,000 high school students play the game.) And amazingly, although the rules have undergone numerous changes over the years, the major tenets of the sport remain the same: three outs per team per inning; 90 feet between the bases; 60 feet, 6 inches from the front edge of the pitcher's rubber to the back point of home plate. Four balls and you're on base. Three strikes and you're out. Fielders record outs in much the same way they've been doing it for over 100 years.

Baseball has a long, rich tradition, and umpires are as much a part of it as players are—although the umpires, of course, play an unobtrusive backdrop to the heroics of the players.

At the same time, the game can't be played without the umpires—and as you doubtless know, good umpiring can make all the difference. Skilled umpires allow the players, coaches and spectators to focus on the game itself, on the efforts and achievements of the players, on the strategies employed by the teams, on the suspense and drama of the competition.

Purpose and Philosophy

You should have three main purposes as an umpire:

1. To ensure fair play by knowing and upholding the rules of the game
2. To minimize risks for the players to the extent that you can
3. To exercise authority in an impartial, firm and controlled manner, as stated in the NFHS Officials Code of Ethics (see page v)

Let's take a moment to consider all three purposes.

Fair Play

Fair play is at the foundation of all games. Nothing will get players, coaches or fans more irate than if they believe that the rules are not being applied correctly and fairly. Competitors want and deserve an equal playing field, created by umpires who have excellent knowledge of the rules and apply them appropriately in all situations.

One of the biggest issues in baseball, in terms of establishing an equal playing field, is calling balls and strikes. Star pitchers at the major-league level sometimes seem to benefit from an expanded strike zone, and star hitters likewise can appear to have a shrunken strike zone. These circumstances are less likely to occur at the high school level, but players, coaches and fans can become incensed when they detect inconsistency in calls. An umpire may call low strikes in one inning, and in the next, call pitches in the same location balls. This lack of uniformity can upset the rhythm of the game and disrupt the attention and focus of the players.

Risk Minimization

Baseball, like all sports, has inherent risks of injury. Two or three fielders converge, at full speed, on a pop-up in shallow centerfield. An outfielder dives headlong for a ball at the fence. A runner slides hard into second base. A pitcher lets loose an 85-mile-per-hour fastball that sails in toward the batter. On and on it goes—the chance for injury is part of the game.

As an umpire you do all you can to minimize those risks and respond appropriately when a player is injured. You can do this in four ways:

- Know and enforce the rules, including those regarding equipment usage. Many of the rules were written to minimize risk to players.
- Inspect the field and report hazardous conditions to management.
- Maintain authority and control in all aspects, including situations when pitchers throw at batters and opponents get in arguments with one another.
- Know how to respond to injuries and emergencies.

Authority

You must exercise authority in an impartial, firm and controlled manner. You can know the rules backward and forward, but if you can't exercise authority, you're going to have a difficult time as an umpire.

Everyone involved in the game is looking to you to make the correct calls and to do so in a manner that doesn't call extra attention to yourself. You want to let all concerned recognize that you know the rules, know how to apply them fairly and impartially, and are in control of every situation.

To gain and maintain authority, then, you must know the rules, be firm and decisive and consistent in your calls, retain control at all times and make every call impartial. When you do this you not only maintain your authority but also uphold the honor and dignity of the profession. Just as players are expected to prepare themselves to play at the top of their game, umpires are expected to exercise appropriate authority in calling the game. Note that this doesn't mean you never blow a call; it means that you never lose control of the game.

What Makes a Good Baseball Official?

Baseball umpires come from all occupations—bankers, insurance agents, business executives, factory workers, postal workers, and on and on. Some have played college or amateur ball; others may have ended their playing careers with youth baseball. Some are just out of high school; others are into retirement.

Despite these differences, good umpires have much in common. They are critical thinkers who can make decisions in the heat of the moment while maintaining their poise. They are able to act as peace-keepers and negotiators, and they know when to step into those roles. They know when and how to stroke an ego without demeaning themselves or harming the integrity of the game. They know when and how to sell a call. They have thick skins and ample patience.

To be a good umpire, you have to blend into the background in one sense yet at the same time be omnipresent and authoritative. You have to maintain control yet keep the game in the players' hands. In the highly emotional arena of sports, you must keep your head about you while all others are losing theirs.

You should be prepared to administer a game in a controlled and professional manner.

Guidelines for Umpire Conduct

- Honor all contracts regardless of possible inconvenience or financial loss.
- Study the rules of the game diligently, observe the work of other umpires and always attempt to improve.
- Remember that although your work as an umpire is important, you must conduct yourself so that spectator attention focuses on the student-athletes playing the game, not you.
- Dress and maintain your appearance in a manner befitting the dignity and importance of the great game of baseball.
- Conduct yourself as a worthy example to players and fans.
- Be fair and unbiased in your decisions, rendering them without regard to the score or next year's contract.
- Give your complete cooperation to the schools that you serve and to the state association that you represent.
- Cooperate and be professional in your association with fellow umpires and do nothing to cause them public embarrassment.
- Be firm but not overbearing, courteous but not ingratiating, positive but never rude, confident but never cocky, friendly but not companionable, and calm but alert.
- Be prepared both physically and mentally to administer the game.
- Do not smoke or use smokeless tobacco on or in the vicinity of the playing field and do not drink any alcoholic beverages on the day of the game.
- Do not give information that a team's future opponent might use.
- Keep in mind that the game is more important than the wishes of any player or coach or the ambitions of any umpire.

No one is perfect. Learn from your mistakes and do your best never to repeat them. You can join the ranks of good umpires by following the 12 prerequisites for good umpiring:

1. Keep in shape.

Although it is important that you have an alert, healthy and sound mind, it is equally important that you keep your body agile and strong. Frequently, you'll need to move quickly to get into the best position to cover a play. Be in good physical shape before the season begins and maintain your conditioning throughout the season.

2. Make calls positively and with good timing.

If you're a novice umpire, be careful about rendering decisions prematurely. Make decisions positively and with good timing but don't be too hasty in calling a play. When you have to run to get into position on a play, it's best to come to a stop where you can see all of the action clearly. Try not to make a decision while in motion. Call all plays with confidence, a practice that you can develop with experience and preparation.

Positive and forceful action does much in getting your call accepted. Cultivate your voice to increase your authority through your spoken word. A strong voice is a valuable asset. Make all calls loudly and clearly so that players of both teams can hear them.

3. Know the rules.

To be a competent umpire, you need to know the rules thoroughly. You make some decisions repeatedly, so with experience some calls will come by reflex. Prepare yourself to make decisions effectively in every circumstance through continual study of all possible situations.

Knowing the rules thoroughly requires constant analytical study. As you study the rules, form mental pictures of plays. These mental images will help you recognize situations when they occur during games, and you'll be better prepared to make the correct calls.

4. Know the mechanics.

Your knowledge of the rules might be enormous, but if your mechanics are poor you will have a hard time getting your calls accepted. When a crew of umpires uses proper mechanics, no play can occur without one of them being in the desired position to see all of the play clearly.

You need to master the mechanics, or play coverage, to be successful. First, you must learn proper positions for various situations, and then you need to practice the coverage so that positioning becomes second nature. Take the best position possible for any given play without being in the way of a player or thrown or batted ball. Let the ball lead you into the play. Look for opportunities to review position and coverage at clinics and to practice the mechanics, whether you're a novice or a veteran.

5. Ignore the fans.

Know that you will be heckled. Every crowd includes some fans who believe that it's not only their right but their duty to insult the umpires. Two traits of good umpires are having a deaf ear toward fans and a thick skin that is impervious to barbs and catcalls.

6. Don't draw undue attention to yourself.

Don't be a showboat; execute your duties without flair. When you take care of your responsibilities with dignity and in conformance with accepted signals and procedures, you'll encourage players and spectators to accept your decisions. Being excessively dramatic doesn't accomplish any good purpose, and such actions frequently cause players to lose confidence in the decisions made because it may seem that an actor made them, not an umpire. Quiet dignity is more effective.

7. Be courteous but don't fraternize.

Be courteous to players and coaches but avoid visiting with them immediately before, during or after a game. Never attempt to coach a player, and don't argue with players, coaches or team representatives. Keep your discussions with these personnel brief and businesslike. A dignified attitude will often preclude or prevent an argument.

8. Hustle and be alert.

To be successful, you have to hustle and be alert. These characteristics are closely associated and are of critical importance. Move briskly, and, when appropriate, urge players to hustle. Keep your head erect and maintain a posture and appearance of one who can properly discharge his or her responsibility. When the ball is pitched, you should never have your arms folded.

9. Call them as you see them.

Your decision-making judgment sharpens with experience. Remember to base your decisions on fact. First, cover the play according to proper procedures and mechanics. Second, and more important, rule on the play exactly as you saw it.

Understand that you will sometime err in your judgment no matter how conscientious and efficient you are and regardless of your position and rules knowledge. When you boot one, simply continue to work to the best of your ability. When you make a rare mistake, you needn't be unduly humbled or embarrassed. And never attempt to even it up after an error. Make each call on its own merits.

10. Be loyal to your crew members.

Through your actions and, when necessary, your words, endorse and support the decisions of your fellow crew members. Be willing to accept responsibility and don't attempt to shift blame to another member of the crew. Don't discuss specific decisions made in a game with the media and don't publicly criticize a fellow umpire.

11. Maintain rapport and respect for other crew members.

Have respect for your fellow umpires. Friendliness and respect for members of the crew (and for the profession) contribute to confidence in one another. Try to support your partner, or partners, throughout the entire contest. When one umpire requests an opinion from another concerning a play, the opinion should be given courteously to the umpire requesting it and to him or her only.

12. Don't infringe on the duties of other crew members.

Make a conscientious effort not to infringe on the duties and responsibilities of fellow umpires. Extreme embarrassment results when umpires make opposing decisions on a play. When umpires observe proper mechanics, conflicting decisions should not occur.

Here are a few final notes on what makes a good umpire:

- Your personal appearance counts. When you look clean and sharp, when your uniform is pressed and in good repair, you will sell your call more often.
- Keep the umpires' dressing room free from visitors. The dressing room is where you and your crewmates prepare yourselves for a game and where you should be able to discuss matters in confidence.
- Do all you can to contribute to or maintain the great traditions of baseball; give your chosen profession or avocation the best possible service. Carry out your assignments to the best of your ability and maintain your integrity at all times.

Officiating at the High School Level

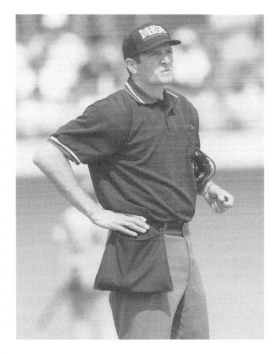

Umpiring baseball at the high school level is similar to umpiring at other levels, but some aspects make the high school experience unique.

You might have umpired at youth levels in which umpires sometimes "coach" players during a game, giving them technique tips or allowing them to bend the rules as they learn the game. At the high school level you neither bend the rules nor coach the players. You simply call the game fairly and authoritatively.

Umpires at the high school level must maintain a businesslike attitude during a game.

Baseball Official's Tools

Several tools can help you excel as an umpire:

- *The current* NFHS Baseball Rules Book. Get it, learn it backward and forward, and sleep with it under your pillow. Know it as well as you possibly can.
- *Umpiring resources.* Use this book and the *Officiating Baseball Mechanics CD (NFHS Edition),* another product of the NFHS Officials Education Program, which shows animated mechanics, as well as magazines and other resources to hone your skills.
- *First-hand experience.* Use every umpiring experience to learn, improve, expand your knowledge of the game and extend your ability to umpire.
- *Second-hand experience.* Learn from watching other good umpires, either in person or on television. Watch their mechanics, how they comport themselves, how they exercise their authority and how they make their calls. Adapt what is useful to your style.
- *Your crewmates.* Learn from their styles and discuss plays and other issues after games. Keep each other sharp in this manner.
- *Clinics and workshops.* Attend as many rules clinics as possible. If none are offered in your area, then suggest to some veteran officials that local umpires should design one of their own. Speak with the schools in your area, and develop a workshop around summer baseball. And don't stop with one clinic or course. Continue to learn throughout your career. Stay sharp. Never become complacent with your learning.
- *A journal.* Use a journal as a self-assessment tool, charting areas for improvement, successes, progress and things learned from each game.
- *Review from others.* Request a fellow umpire from your local officials' chapter to come to watch you and comment on your work.
- *Self-review.* Have a friend videotape a game so that you can review it later.
- *Pre- and postgame meetings.* Meetings before and after games are key learning times for umpires, especially beginners. If you're a new umpire or even if you're a veteran, there's no shame in asking more experienced umpires for advice.

Another difference among levels is the number of umpires used. Sometimes at youth levels you have only one umpire; sometimes you have two. At the major-league level you have four (and six during playoffs). At the high school level you typically operate in two-umpire crews, although on occasion you might find yourself in a three-umpire or four-umpire crew. In chapters 5 through 7, respectively, you'll learn how to operate in these types of crews.

Rules vary as well. For example, at the high school level, starting players can re-enter the game once as long as they hit in the same spot in the order; an intentional walk can be given without pitching; a fielder without the ball cannot fake a tag; and pop-up slides and slides in which the runner's raised leg is higher than the fielder's knee are illegal. In major-league baseball none of those rules apply. You will note many other differences. For example, in college baseball, a pitcher can turn his shoulders to check on a runner on base. In high school that action is illegal. See your *NFHS Baseball Rules Book* for other differences.

As a high school baseball umpire you can join the NFHS Officials Association. Through your state officials' association, you can receive assignments, attend annual rules meetings to learn new rules and hone your techniques and other skills, and attend clinics throughout the year. Take advantage of applying for membership in both the NFHS Officials Association and your state organization to continue to learn and develop your skills as an umpire.

CHAPTER 2

GAME PROCEDURES AND RESPONSIBILITIES

In the previous chapter we considered the main purposes of umpires, what makes a good umpire, and the tools that umpires use to continue to develop their skills and grow in their profession. In this chapter we'll begin to get into the nitty-gritty of your responsibilities as an umpire and procedures to follow before, during and after games.

Plate and Field Umpire Responsibilities

Here we'll give an overview of the general responsibilities of the umpire-in-chief (the plate umpire) and the field umpire or base umpires. We'll later build on this foundation by discussing, in chapters 3 through 7, the mechanics of plate and field umpires and how to operate in two-, three- and four-umpire crews.

Umpire-in-Chief

If you are a plate umpire you are designated as the umpire-in-chief and will be stationed behind home plate to rule on balls, strikes, fair and foul balls, and make all decisions on the batter, other than those delegated to the base umpire.

You are responsible for announcing, "Play" and for giving the hand signal to start the game or resume play. You should start a game only after you are sure that representatives of both teams clearly understand the pregame discussion of ground rules.

As umpire-in-chief you will determine if lights need to be turned on. If possible you should do that before the beginning of an inning. You also have the sole authority to forfeit a game or call a game if conditions become unfit for play. Remember, the base umpire is an excellent resource when considering the field conditions.

Whenever the base umpire goes into the outfield to rule on a play, you must step into the infield and watch base runners as they advance, observing whether they tagged up on caught fly balls. Be careful, however, not to leave home plate unguarded in case you must make a decision there.

The umpire-in-chief has several additional responsibilities:

- Ejecting a player or coach, clearing a bench, sending a coach from the field or restricting a coach to the bench or dugout if necessary
- Announcing each substitution
- Penalizing for rule infractions such as balks, interference, baserunning infractions, delay, unwarranted disputing of decisions and unsporting conduct
- Making final decisions on points not covered by the rules
- Keeping a written record of conferences charged to defensive and offensive teams and notifying the respective coach each time a conference is charged to his team
- Keeping a lineup card and recording all substitutes, courtesy runner participation and team warnings
- Reporting protests when a game is played under the auspices of an organization that permits filing of protests

For a more detailed list of the responsibilities of the umpire-in-chief, see the current *NFHS Baseball Rules Book*.

Field Umpire or Base Umpires

A field umpire is part of a two-umpire crew and aids the umpire-in-chief in administering the rules. If you are a field umpire you will make all decisions on the bases except those reserved for the umpire-in-chief.

When more than one field umpire is used, they are referred to as base umpires and their normal positions are behind first and third bases on a three-crew system and behind first, second and third bases on a four-crew system.

If you are a base umpire positioned to cover a ball in the outfield hit toward a foul line, and the ball is hit toward that foul line, you should run to the outfield area to make the ruling and to signal your decision. Stay close to the foul line to make the fair or foul ruling. Make the fair or foul call first and then determine whether the fielder trapped or caught the ball.

You will also make the call when you are stationed near first or third base and a batted ball hits near a foul line beyond that base. The exception here is when a ball is hit so hard that you must move rapidly for self-protection and you therefore lose sight of the ball. The umpire-in-chief has the fair or foul call up to the front edge of the bag.

Common Responsibilities and Communication

Any umpire can call a balk, signal a delayed dead ball or call time-out. Avoid declaring time-out, however, when a play is about to occur.

As noted in chapter 1, don't call plays while on the run. Although you certainly want to get the best possible view of the action, you cannot be on top of every play. Move as rapidly as possible to get a good angle and then stop before the action occurs. Your vision is much better when you are stationary than when you are running.

A stationary position will help you focus on the game's action.

A progression for making a call in a normal situation is the following:

1. Is the ball fair or foul?
2. Is there a catch?
3. What is the outcome of the play?

Crew members must develop a communication system to use among themselves. Appropriate signs enable umpires to let fellow crew members know, unobtrusively, their judgment of a play. Agree on a simple system of signals before the game starts.

One example of the necessity of communication between umpires occurs on a check swing when whether the batter offered at the pitch is in question. The principle now universally accepted is that if the batter swings the barrel end of the bat so that it is in front of his body or ahead of it, it is a strike. Occasionally, however, the plate umpire's vision may be blocked. If you are the plate umpire in that situation, you might seek the opinion of one of your fellow umpires before making your decision, even though you are the sole judge of balls and strikes and your decisions are final. To seek your crew member's opinion, you point with your left hand to the base umpire from whom you seek help and ask, "Did he go?"

That umpire will respond with a strike signal if he or she feels that the batter swung. If the base umpire feels that the batter checked his swing in time, he or she will quickly give a safe signal and call out, "No, he did not!"

That's just one example of umpire signaling, which is an important aspect of communication by umpires. By using signals, umpires relay decisions to players, coaches and spectators. The adopted umpires' signals are dignified, informative and meaningful; make sure you use them. Poorly executed and unauthorized signals serve only to confuse. The manner in which you give a signal can determine its acceptance by players, coaches and fans.

Of course, a player or coach may at times have reasonable doubt about a call you have made—for example, whether a runner is safe or out or whether a ball is fair or foul. The coach or team captain can ask that the correct ruling be made, and you can ask another umpire for information before making a final decision. Make sure not to criticize or interfere with another umpire's decision unless the umpire who made the decision asks you for help.

Pregame Procedures and Responsibilities

Your responsibilities as an umpire begin well before the game. You should arrive early, ideally being at the field at least 30 minutes before the game. Because high school games are played after school, you might have to leave work early or might be just getting off work. You may not be able to arrive more than 30 minutes before the game, although some umpires make it a point to arrive an hour before game time. Regardless, don't arrive so close to game time that you must neglect your pregame duties. With this in mind, make sure to plan for the unexpected, such as traffic jams or car problems, and allow yourself ample time to get to the field to tend to your pregame duties. See the Pregame Checklist for your main pregame duties.

Pregame Checklist

- ❏ Notify management immediately upon your arrival.
- ❏ Gather with your crewmates for a pregame conference to prepare for the game. Discuss positioning, how to deal with timing plays, how to handle assistance on checked swings and foul balls, and ground rules.
- ❏ Closely examine the playing field, making certain that it is properly marked, that the pitcher's plate is legal in every respect and that you are familiar with the boundaries, fences and screens. As you examine the field, note all obstacles that could create dead-ball situations. Look for potential safety problems or risks. Your crew should tour the field together so that you can consider any points or questions concerning safety and ground rules and report the conclusion to the appropriate individuals.
- ❏ Ten minutes before the scheduled game time, move onto the field. Check the equipment of each team to make sure that it is legal and safe. The plate umpire should check the visitors; a field umpire should check the home team. You should thoroughly inspect bats, helmets, and catcher's mask and helmet combinations. Batting helmets and catcher's helmets must have the National Operating Committee on Standards for Athletic Equipment (NOCSAE) seal. Bring to the attention of the coach any illegal or unsafe equipment. That equipment should be stored so that players cannot use it during the game.
- ❏ At least five minutes before the scheduled starting time, you and your crew should meet team coaches or team captains at home plate for a pregame conference to check lineups (home team first) and discuss ground rules and any other pertinent matters. Ask coaches whether all their players are legally and properly equipped, and share your expectation that they exhibit good sporting behavior. Don't forget to check about designated-hitter (DH) or speed-up rules. If the game involves tournament play, you may have to toss a coin to determine which team is the home team if the tournament manager has not previously made this determination.
- ❏ Make sure that the official scorer has been provided with copies of the two starting batting orders after you have inspected the cards to eliminate any errors in recording. Check the data with the scorer and correct any errors in transmission.
- ❏ Briefly discuss with the official scorer such matters as the proper batting orders and the appearance of pinch hitters and substitutes. This matter is particularly important in interscholastic games because of the re-entry and designated-hitter rules.

From *Officiating Baseball* by ASEP, 2004, Champaign, IL: Human Kinetics.

Just as players must prepare to perform before each game, so must umpires. Use the time before the game to get comfortable with your crew, to make sure that you each know your responsibilities, to iron out any positioning issues and to familiarize yourself with the ground rules and any other rules that are in question.

Postgame Procedures and Responsibilities

When the game is over, take care of your equipment. The umpire-in-chief should return the baseballs to the home management. Then leave the field with the other crew members. Don't discuss the game with anyone; get off the field quickly. If you have to change clothes, move to an off-site location to do so. Don't give fans or others the chance to harass you about calls made in a game that's over.

PART II

BASEBALL OFFICIATING MECHANICS

CHAPTER 3

PLATE UMPIRE MECHANICS

Understanding your responsibilities and knowing how to carry them out, which we covered in chapter 2, is fundamental to your success as an umpire. But just as important is your knowledge of the mechanics of umpiring and your ability to execute it.

In this chapter we'll cover mechanics specific to the plate umpire. As a plate umpire you'll be involved in literally every pitch and play during a game. The mechanics presented in this chapter will help you be efficient and effective in your plate umpiring skills. We'll present mechanics in these areas:

- Preparing for the pitch
- Making calls
- Responding to balls
- Communicating on the field
- Establishing your reputation
- Evaluating additional issues

Preparing for the Pitch

As a plate umpire preparing for the pitch is vital to your ability to make good calls. You must be in proper position and have an unobstructed view of the plate. Let's look more closely at these and a few other items.

Position and Stance

In preparing for the pitch position and stance are critical to good umpiring because they will be determining factors in whether or not your calls are accurate. Here we'll look at the importance of your position in relation to the pitcher and catcher and how to position your hands.

Position in Relation to the Catcher

As a plate umpire you'll work to the side and rear of the catcher. Which side you'll work on depends on the batter. With left-handed batters, you'll work to the catcher's right; with right-handers, you'll work to the catcher's left. Avoid positioning yourself too far forward where you are in danger of being hit by the bat on the follow-through. Remember to take advantage of your best available protection—the catcher.

To work the plate consistently, take the same position behind the catcher on every pitch. After the catcher has settled down to receive the pitch, assume your stance—the one that will give you the best perspective from which to judge the pitch. How you place your feet is crucial to stance. The most common method is a catcherlike crouch behind the catcher.

Whether you work the scissors, the box or the knee stance (see figures 3.1-3.3), your head should be in the same position every time. Your chin should be at the top of the catcher's head, with your head slightly behind and in the slot between the catcher and the batter (see figure 3.4 on page 24). If the position of the catcher or batter makes it impossible for you to see the pitch, adjust as well as you can. As a last resort, move above and directly behind the catcher's head. You will be able to see the corners but will lose some perspective on the low pitch. Go back to normal position as soon as the batter or catcher allows it.

Seeing the pitch well sometimes depends on the catcher. His stance just before the pitch may cause a problem in your following the flight of the ball. The better the catcher and pitcher, the easier and more enjoyable

FIGURE 3.1   Plate umpire in the scissors stance.

FIGURE 3.2   Plate umpire in the box stance.

FIGURE 3.3   Plate umpire in the knee stance.

FIGURE 3.4 Correct plate umpire body position.

it is to umpire, because they are consistent in how they work and you know what to expect.

Position in Relation to the Pitcher

For best protection, face the pitcher. Don't expose the unprotected side of your body. Point your toes toward the pitcher so that your foot is not angled to the flight of the ball. Otherwise, your instep will be vulnerable to the pitch or a foul ball. In addition, the outside padded tongue of the plate shoe offers considerably less protection if you angle your foot. Wear a mask with extended throat protection because the inside protector does not protect the neck or throat.

Hands

Positioning of your hands is critical. You can protect your hands with a right-handed batter at the plate by placing your left elbow in the inside of the left leg when you're down in the squat position (see figure 3.5). Your hands are down behind the catcher and loose so that they will give. Don't put your hand on your knee. If the ball hits your hand in that position, there is no give. The bones in the hand break easily.

Many umpires rest their forearms on the top of their thighs instead of tucking their elbows inside the leg, but we don't recommend this position because it leaves your elbows unprotected. Touching the catcher with your hands is a bad habit. Some catchers will tell you to move back, that you bother them and interfere with their freedom of movement. If this happens, respect the catcher's request and give him a little more space. Place yourself a comfortable distance from the catcher but close enough that you have a good view of the strike zone and the plate area.

If you are getting bona fide criticism on your ball and strike calls from the pitcher, catcher or manager and you know that you're having difficulties, you'll want to show some response. For example, if you're having problems with the catcher's positioning, ask him to adjust if possible. If you are having difficulty with the pitcher's positioning, speak to him through the catcher. If the coach is becoming a point of contention, speak with him in between innings so that he is aware that you have acknowledged his concerns. But be sure to differentiate between legitimate complaints and mere whining.

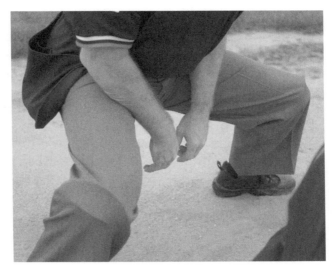

FIGURE 3.5   Correct plate umpire hand position.

View

Your view of the pitch is, of course, critical to your ability to call balls and strikes. Here, we'll consider your line of sight and the strike zone.

Line of Sight

As you set up, place your head so that your chin is at the top of the catcher's head. Establish a good line of sight. When you're down in the squat position, your line of sight should be somewhat over the left shoulder of the catcher when the batter is right-handed. After the pitch has been released, don't move to follow it. Your view over the plate should be complete. Don't let the catcher's head block your view of an outside pitch. If it does, adjust your stance to get an unobstructed view. The squat style seems to make outside pitches harder to call, but if you have a long torso you can use this position successfully. Just be sure not to squat so low that you miss the outside pitch because the catcher's body blocks it.

If you are working the inside-protector style (with your head inside the slot between the catcher and the batter) and are getting hit with foul balls too often, you are probably working too high and not taking advantage of your best available protection, the catcher.

Another problem with the inside-protector style occurs with a sidearm left-handed pitcher and a left-handed batter who crowds the plate. This combination makes it difficult to pick up the pitch until it is well on its way. Your time to size it up becomes much too brief. In this case, reposition your head to achieve the best view possible.

Strike Zone

The *NFHS Baseball Rules Book* defines the strike zone: over home plate, with the top of the zone being halfway between the batter's shoulders and the waistline and the bottom of the zone being the knees when the batter assumes his normal stance.

As an umpire you have the best vantage point as well as the sole responsibility of determining whether the ball is in the strike zone. To establish a consistent strike zone, you might want to develop reference points for the inside strike and the top of the strike zone. For example, for a right-handed batter if you are in a slotted stance, you might use your left leg to establish the inside zone. When squatting behind the catcher, use a reference point on the mask to establish the height of the zone.

Related Matters

You should consider a couple other matters when preparing for the pitch. These are the batter's position in the box and a malady that occasionally affects plate umpires—flinching.

Batter in Box

Be sure that the batter is in the batter's box when establishing his position. Quickly glance at his bat to be sure it is legal. Take note of his stance to establish his particular strike zone.

Flinching

Flinching is an occasional problem for some umpires. Many umpires have worked consecutive games without a hint of a flinch and then suddenly had it occur. Flinching can irritate you far more than it affects your actual umpiring skills. If the flinching is so pronounced that fans or players notice it, umpires become more concerned, and rightly so, about their image.

A common remedy for flinching is to force yourself to wait as long as you can before getting into your stance just before the pitch. This method shortens the amount of time of stressful concentration through the release of the pitch and the hit.

Making Calls

As a plate umpire you will make lots of calls—not only on balls and strikes but also on a variety of other plays. In this section we'll look at proper mechanics, calling pitches, calling outs and making other calls.

Proper Mechanics

Here we'll look at how you time and make your strike call. These are important aspects of selling your call.

Timing of Calling the Pitch

An important part of the mechanics of plate umpiring is proper timing. Don't make your call too soon or too late. Be conscious of your timing. If you're off, it's better to be a little slow than to make snap judgments. Let the pitch hit the catcher's mitt, then delay slightly before you strike call the pitch. A good way to slow your timing is to remind yourself mentally to lock in before each pitch. Your timing on making calls for strikes and balls should be the same.

You might at times notice that your timing is deteriorating. Here's a tip if you notice that you're calling pitches too quickly. When getting down in the squat position, place the fingers of your strike hand into the bend of your left knee. When you are completely down in the final position, make sure that your fingers are locked into the bend so that you can't pull them out. The only way to release the fingers to make the strike call is to start to stand up. This extra second keeps you from making the strike motion too quickly. You can also grab the inside of the left pant leg and hold on tightly. This method is largely psychological, but it often helps.

Strike Motion

When the pitch is a strike, start the upward movement of the strike arm (your right arm) out in front of you as you begin to stand up. (Some umpires step backward one step. Doing so is OK, depending to some extent on how close you are to the catcher. Sometimes you can't bring your strike arm forward without hitting the catcher.) Bring your arm up in front of you for at least half of the strike call. Bring your fist up to eye level or higher, letting your arm bend naturally for a simple strike (see figure 3.6). Don't have your thumb up in the air.

FIGURE 3.6   Plate umpire calling a strike.

For a bit more emphasis, you can chop the fist down slightly to the left or right. For a third-strike call, alter the mechanics to make the call different from other strike calls. You can move your fist to the right or left to give the emphasis needed. Some umpires indicate the number of strikes with their fingers at the end of the strike call.

Bringing your arm and fist forward and up rather than to the right and up in the first part of the strike call lets all who are on the left side of the diamond, as well as those on the right, see the strike motion. Don't end the motion with the fist too low because your body will hide it from those on the opposite side.

On third strikes, or other called strikes that are crucial, you can step back with either foot and bring the fist down across your body like pounding a nail. This action is just one emphatic style of calling a strike.

Remember, on swinging third strikes, the batter has already communicated the drama of the moment to all. A perfunctory motion is enough. But you are the communicator on the called third strike, and thus this call needs your emphasis.

Calling Pitches

Your motion is important in calling pitches; so is your voice. Here we'll look at how to make your oral calls and whether you should go into explanations of your calls.

Oral Calls

Call out called strikes and balls. On swinging strikes, though, say nothing. Just raise your fist and point to the batter, because the action itself clearly communicates the message, unless it's a checked swing.

On the first called strike, call out, "Strike!" loudly. On the second strike, if it's a called strike, make it louder. On the third strike, if it's a called strike, make the call loudest of all and perhaps use some body movement to make it different from strikes one and two. In addition, when the pitch is a ball, call, "Ball!" loudly enough for the infielders to hear.

There is a reason for calling balls and strikes audibly. If you don't call the ball aloud, it's harder to maintain proper timing. Vary your calls of nonswinging strikes in intensity, tone and length, depending on their importance in the game.

Explaining Calls

Don't routinely explain your ball and strike calls, such as saying, "Ball! Low," "Ball! Inside" or "Strike! Caught the corner." If the catcher asks where a certain pitch was, tell him. But if the catcher repeatedly asks, "Where was the pitch?" you should tell him that you're not going to explain every pitch to him. Tell him that he is perfectly aware of where he caught the pitch—low, outside and so on. From that point on, don't discuss pitches.

A batter will at times inquire if what he swung at and missed was a strike. Give him the information he asks for. For example, tell him, "No, it was a little high," if that is what you thought. Make it short and don't editorialize, but it's OK to respond to such requests from players because it doesn't violate any principles of communication between umpire and player. Even major-league umpires respond to such requests.

Style

You will probably umpire many games trying various methods to come up with a style that communicates well and fits you. Watch other umpires. Try techniques that appeal to you. If they work for you, use them. Experiment and use the style that suits you best. Each style is synonymous with personality, flare and effectiveness, and you should be comfortable with your style in conducting your officiating duties.

Making Other Calls

Your calls—whether for safe or out calls, fair or foul calls, balks or illegal pitches, or any other calls—should be consistent and clear.

Out Calls

Out calls vary little. Your arm movement is virtually the same, differing only slightly because of stance.

The out call starts low and ends nearly in a stand-up position. Make the call with your right hand, with your elbow straight out from your shoulder and bent at 90 degrees with your fist clinched. If you remove your mask before you give the out sign, you hold it, of course, in your left hand (see figure 3.7).

As always, fit the emphasis to the closeness of the play or the game situation. Match your voice to your body language and make sure both fit the action.

FIGURE 3.7 Plate umpire making an emphatic out call after removing mask.

Fair or Foul Calls

Avoid ambiguous fair or foul calls and make sure that you use completely different gestures when you call a batted ball fair or foul.

For the foul call, you will signal the ball foul by first putting both hands over your head and then motioning to foul territory (see figure 3.8). Yell, "Foul!" as emphatically as you gesture. If the call is crucial to the game or barely foul, yell, "Foul! Foul! Foul!" Using any other words might cause the call to be misunderstood. The earflaps of helmets and crowd noise make hearing difficult for players.

Calling, "Foul!" halts all play and the ball automatically becomes dead. The call is not reversible so don't make the foul call prematurely. Declare the ball dead as soon as it becomes dead, but don't make the foul call prematurely. Remember, the ball is dead as soon as the umpire calls it foul. If the ball is in foul territory between home and first base or home and third base, don't call the ball foul until it settles on foul territory or touches an umpire, player or any object foreign to the natural ground (such as players' equipment or media equipment).

FIGURE 3.8   Plate umpire calling a foul.

When you judge the ball to be fair, use no oral call but point toward fair territory while keeping your eye on the ball. Runners tend to think "foul" when they hear an umpire make an oral call in a fair or foul situation.

On long fly balls hit down the line that are the plate umpire's call, immediately remove your mask. Sprint down the baseline following the ball as far as you can before it is time to make a decision. Be on the foul line if possible and remember to stop before you make the call. On sharp line drives, you may not have time to remove your mask or move for a better look. Get the best look you can and make the call.

Plays at the Plate

For plays at the plate, observe the runner touching or retouching third. Position yourself on the third-base line extended past home plate. Adjust to either side of the plate, depending on the play. If a foul ball requires you to leave the plate with the catcher to observe the catch, you have the responsibility to observe a runner tagging at third. Before moving into position to make the call, remain behind the catcher, adjusting a few steps to either side depending on the throw and the runner. Establish a clear line of sight through the play and make sure that neither the catcher nor the runner screens you from the play (see figure 3.9).

FIGURE 3.9   Plate umpire in good position to make a call at the plate.

On a play in which the runner misses home plate and the catcher misses tagging the runner, make no call. If the catcher then tags the runner before the runner touches the plate, call the runner out for missing the plate. If the defense makes a dead-ball appeal, call the runner out. If the runner misses the plate, the catcher misses the tag and never applies one, and the runner never touches home but trots back to the dugout, the run scores if no valid appeal is made.

Balk and Illegal Pitch

When a balk occurs, throw up your hands to signify that the ball is dead and call, "Balk!" Award each runner one base (see figure 3.10).

Likewise, when an illegal pitch occurs, throw up your hands and call, "Illegal pitch!" On an illegal pitch, the ball is dead and a ball is awarded the batter.

FIGURE 3.10   Plate umpire awarding a base to a runner following a balk.

Responding to Balls

As plate umpire you'll have plenty of calls to make around the plate. Here are proper mechanics for situations at the plate and away from the plate.

At the Plate

Obviously, plenty of action is going on at and around the plate. Here we'll consider the catcher's space, foul tips, batted balls hitting the batter, foul tips and passed balls.

Catcher's Space

Give the catcher room. Keeping out of the way of the catcher on a foul ball can be tricky. If you understand the basic moves of the properly taught catcher, staying clear of him is easier.

Not all catchers cover fouls in the standard way. Try to figure out, as best you can, what a catcher is likely to do. Give him adequate room to do it, and if possible, enough space to do the unpredictable. Never put your hand on the catcher's back.

When a right-hander fouls off an inside pitch, the catcher should turn to his left because the fouled ball usually goes over his left shoulder. Therefore, you should be ready to turn to the left with the catcher.

When a right-hander fouls an outside pitch, the ball goes up over the catcher's right shoulder. The properly trained catcher automatically whirls to his right in this case, as does the properly trained umpire. Simply reverse the movements when a left-handed hitter is at the plate. Just make sure you give the catcher enough space to operate in.

Keep your eye on the catcher, not the foul ball. His job is to catch the foul; yours is to stay out of his way while following the action. As the catcher moves to find and catch the ball, move with him but maintain a safe distance in case he changes direction. If the catcher runs to the fence, dugout or elsewhere, follow him. Being close to this kind of play allows you to make the call easier.

Foul Tips

Indicate foul tips. When the catcher legally catches a foul tip, give a foul-tip signal by brushing the palms of your hands above your head as they pass each other (see figure 3.11). Quickly repeat the sign two or three times if you wish. This gesture accomplishes several things: It informs fans of the foul tip, it alerts runners that the ball is alive and it gives meticulous scorers the information they need for the scorebook. Most of the time foul tips can't be detected at a distance. If the foul tip is uncaught, it becomes a foul ball.

Batted Ball Hitting Batter

React immediately to a batted ball that hits the batter. When the ball goes from the bat directly to the dirt and then strikes the batter or catcher, immediately kill the play by throwing your arms up and calling, "Foul!" (see figure 3.12).

FIGURE 3.11   Plate umpire calling a foul tip.

Only the front inside corner of the batter's box is in fair territory. A ticked ball is almost certain to be in foul territory by the time it hits the batter. Should the ball make contact with the batter near the fair corner of the box, it's often difficult to judge. Most umpires automatically call such a ball a foul. Those involved expect such a call, though they might give you a little trouble on the rare occasion that the ball spins its way into fair territory after you've made the call.

Passed Ball

On a passed ball with a runner on third, a play at home is likely, so be alert. Remove your mask quickly and set yourself at a right angle to the catcher's throw. This gives you a good angle on the play at home (see figure 3.13). Most important, watch the ball and the catcher going after it; otherwise you don't know where he will be when he makes the throw. Make sure the catcher gets the ball and makes the throw, and follow the flight of the ball as you turn to watch the play. Be careful because a badly thrown ball could hit you if you turn too quickly. Take adequate time on this call.

FIGURE 3.12 Plate umpire calling foul after a batted ball hits the batter in the box.

FIGURE 3.13 Plate umpire in good position to make a call as the catcher retrieves and throws a passed ball.

When you are certain that the play is complete, make your call emphatic with appropriate body language. After all, your call takes its importance from the importance of the play.

Away From the Plate

Although plenty of action goes on around the plate, much takes place away from the plate as well. Here we'll consider your duties on ground balls, slow rollers and fly balls.

Ground Ball to the Infield

As plate umpire your duties don't end when the batter hits the ball. First, watch to see if the batter runs. If he does, move out from behind the catcher to get a better look at the play.

On a ground ball hit to the infield, head toward first base, either down the running lane or on the infield grass. Try to get at least 10 to 15 feet from home plate, the farther the better, but stop in time to watch the play at first. This initial hustle shortens the distance to the action and gives you a better vantage point from which to see runner infractions. Sometimes what starts as a routine play develops into a difficult situation for the base umpire if his or her view becomes blocked. If you have moved properly, you will be where you can see what is happening and be of assistance to your partner, if help is requested. Be alert for the first baseman who pulls his foot off the base too soon.

Slow Roller

A play that makes the plate umpire hustle is the batted slow roller down a foul line. Stay on top of the slow roller; don't hesitate. Get out from behind the plate and as close to the ball as possible without getting so close that you interfere with the fielding of the ball. You can take your mask off on this play if you have time.

Fly Ball

On a fly ball hit to the outfield, go farther than you do for an infield grounder. Many times you go out as far as the pitcher's mound to watch the catch in the outfield. Note whether the ball is caught, trapped or dropped. You have the job of observing the catch if the base umpire elects not to go to the outfield. The base umpire has the job of seeing whether the runner touches the bases. But don't get too far from home plate if a play may occur there.

When the base umpire goes to the outfield to follow the play on a long, hard-hit fly ball near the right-field foul line, move quickly to the infield, circling the pitcher's mound for a possible play at second while making sure that the batter-runner touches first. (By going around the mound, you eliminate the possibility of stumbling over it.) If the runner attempts to reach second base, your hustle will put you there before the runner arrives, right on top of the play. After all, the runner had to go the long route while you took a shortcut. Done right, covering second in this way is beautiful. The play will earn you respect and contribute to your reputation. You won't often have to do this, but when the situation arises, be ready.

With no runners on base, be prepared to rule on trapped balls hit to left field. The base umpire will rule on balls hit to center and right. On all routine fly balls, move near the pitcher's mound and shout, "I'm going out!" so that your partner can hear you. The base umpire moves into the infield. If the fielder drops the ball, the base umpire then checks to see if the batter-runner tags first base and that the first baseman does not obstruct the runner. He or she then moves for a possible play at first or second.

When the base umpire moves to the outfield to rule on a possible trap, you must rule on plays at all bases and should move to the center of the diamond where you can move in any direction. After the base umpire makes a ruling, you should head for home plate to make a ruling on any throw made there.

Communicating on the Field

Umpiring is all about communicating. You communicate balls and strikes, whether runners are out or safe, whether balls are fair or foul, and on and on. You communicate with your fellow umpires, with players and managers, and, through your signals and calls, with fans. In this section we'll look at your communication with other umpires, with players and coaches, and in handling complaints.

Communicating With Other Umpires

Proper communication begins with your fellow crew members. Here we'll talk about two aspects of that communication.

Umpire Unity
Don't openly disagree with crew members. If you don't agree with a call your partner makes, wait until after the game and discuss the call or play with him or her in private.

You can avoid many potential differences with crew members by discussing troublesome rules and ground rules privately before the game. Working with the same partner in many games makes this and many other aspects of umpiring easier (see chapter 2 for more on working with fellow crew members). Of course, consulting with fellow umpires on certain plays or when your view is blocked is appropriate.

Remember, you are a team, and coaches, players and spectators usually judge you as such. A partner who uses bad judgment reflects on you. Conversely, if he or she is a good umpire and has earned a high level of respect, some of this respect will transfer to you.

Infield Fly

The infield-fly situation frequently arises in a game, and when it does, umpires need to communicate with each other. You should have a signal to give one another before the pitch is made to acknowledge that the infield-fly rule is in effect. One umpire gives the sign and the other umpires acknowledge, usually by reciprocating with the same sign. You can use any of a variety of signals. Pick one that is not so conspicuous that players immediately recognize it. Your purpose is to communicate to your fellow umpires, not to coach the players inadvertently.

When a hit ball is judged to be an infield fly, give the infield-fly signal by raising your right hand over-head and pointing your index finger at the ball (see figure 3.14). At the same time yell, "Infield fly! If fair, batter's out!" Include "If fair" regardless of the trajectory of the ball in relation to the foul line. This habitual qualification takes care of the fly that ends up foul and causes no problem when the fly is obviously fair.

Usually the plate umpire calls the infield fly first, but a field umpire can make the call first if the plate umpire hasn't made the call when the field umpire judges the hit ball to be an infield fly. Each umpire is responsible for making the infield fly call. When your partner calls the infield fly, regardless of how you see it, you have to go along. This approach preserves the essential image of umpire unity and discourages players from challenging the call.

Be sure to call to your partner when you will be covering third base. Doing this is important because with your partner's back

FIGURE 3.14   Plate umpire calling an infield fly.

to third, he or she needs to know you will be there. The communication should be just loud enough for your partner to hear.

Communicating With Players and Coaches

Obviously, your umpiring must communicate clearly to players and coaches. Here are some aspects of that communication.

Infield Fly

In communicating the infield-fly rule to players, don't be in a hurry to make the call; make it as the ball starts downward. This method informs the runner or runners in time and enables you to judge whether an infielder can catch the ball with ordinary effort. If an outfielder catches a ball that an infielder could have caught with ordinary effort, the infield-fly rule is still in effect.

Showing the Count

If you feel that the information is needed, extend your fingers to indicate the number of balls and strikes. This method is especially useful at amateur ball fields that don't have a prompt and accurate operator of the ball and strike display or have no scoreboard at all.

If you do show the strike count with your fingers, do it so that all can see. Players must know the count. If the board has it wrong, announce the correct count and show it with your fingers.

Batters

On ball four, don't award the walk by pointing to first base. This gesture doesn't really help the batter. Simply announcing, "Ball four!" is sufficient. A batter who has his head in the game knows the count. If he doesn't move toward first, don't prompt him by pointing. Let him stand there a moment or two. He and his coach will both become aware that he should be revising his awareness of the game situation pitch by pitch. Any embarrassment at having to ask when you've called ball four will teach the batter to be more attentive.

Pitchers

A pitcher will at times be unhappy with your call. As a result, he might approach the area of home plate to voice his objections. Being inexperienced or overwrought, he might not realize that technically no player or coach can object to a ball or strike call. In addition, umpires have an unwritten understanding that no player, especially the pitcher, can come to the area of home plate to argue about the call of a pitch.

In high school baseball the pitcher may not know this, or he may know but hasn't learned to discipline himself. If you feel you must communicate with the pitcher, share your concerns with the catcher and send him to the mound. Explain to the catcher that it is his duty to keep his pitcher on the mound and to tone down the pitcher's display of displeasure at adverse calls. Be firm but polite.

Time-Out

You will frequently have to call time-out. Sometimes only a few players in the immediate area need to be aware that time has been called. On other occasions, everyone—players and fans alike—needs to know that time has been called. No umpire has the voice to accomplish this, so when you call time-out, use the time-out sign of throwing up both hands over your head, together with a loud, "Time!" (see figure 3.15).

Don't overuse time-outs, however. Don't call time when doing so would prevent the completion of a play. Let play continue unless you have a valid reason for calling time. (Two situations that may warrant a time-out are after a bang-bang play at first or a close play at the plate. After such plays end, players may need time to collect themselves or make sure that they're not hurt.) Don't grant a player's request for time unless he has a bona fide reason.

When a time-out is not necessary, you may delay play without calling time. If a batter asks for time to get set with no runners on, simply tell him that you will not let the pitcher pitch until he is ready. If the pitcher subsequently begins any action to pitch, you may then raise your hand and kill the play. Remember, the "Do not pitch" signal creates a dead ball, which must then be properly made alive. When the batter is set and everyone is ready, announce, "Play!" and point to the pitcher.

When the batter steps out of the batter's box unexpectedly and you decide to give him time—when you judge you can stop the action before the pitcher goes into his motion—quickly throw up your hands and yell, "Time!" When added

FIGURE 3.15   Plate umpire calling time-out.

emphasis is needed, take a few quick side steps. This movement gets you out where you are more visible and shows that you do not intend to call a pitch if the pitcher makes one. Calling time quickly and clearly either stops the pitcher comfortably or lets the pitcher make a soft pitch if he can't stop.

Once time is called or the ball becomes dead, the ball becomes live when

1. the pitcher holds the ball in a legal pitching position (provided the pitcher has engaged the pitcher's plate),
2. the batter and the catcher are in their respective boxes and
3. you call, "Play!" and give the appropriate hand signal.

With time back in, the pitcher is under no more obligation to pitch than he would be ordinarily.

Handling Complaints

Players and coaches will complain, no matter how well you call a game. Here is some advice on how to handle complaints and confrontations.

Catchers and Managers

Be prepared to handle complaints by catchers and managers. Ordinarily, umpires permit the catcher to make remarks in a mild, quiet tone as long as he is facing the pitcher. Never let the catcher turn around to protest more than once. Warn him. A good way to do this without embarrassing him is to brush the plate, look him in the eye and explain your dissatisfaction. Take sterner action the next time it happens.

Managers who constantly protest strike calls from the bench set a bad example in field manners. Deal subtly with their actions. One way is to talk to them between innings, telling them they should show some restraint. If they feel they have a legitimate gripe, they should not be ill-mannered in presenting it. Players will seize upon their manager's manners, good or bad. Mangers should come to you between innings in a respectful manner to make their point. If they choose not to use this method and persist in hollering and physically displaying their objections, take appropriate action. (This means restricting coaches to the dugout area and, with the next infraction, ejecting them.) Be sure that what you do is necessary and just. Use your best judgment and then act.

Whenever you deal with managers or players, don't purposely embarrass them. Don't look for trouble; it will come without any help from you. The best way to handle conflict when it comes is to remain calm and civil.

Confrontation

Don't argue with a coach. If a coach questions a judgment call, say something like, "Coach, that's a judgment call and that's the way I see it. Let's play ball!" If he questions a rules interpretation, explain your ruling. Don't prolong conversation; resume play. If you have any doubt about your ruling, don't be afraid to ask a fellow umpire—and if you are incorrect, change your ruling. This discussion with your fellow umpire should be private and away from coaches and players. Keep cool at all times.

Here are a couple of ways that you can avoid trouble between innings. When you have a difference of opinion on balls and strikes with the team that just batted, do not go toward them as they take the field. If you do, they could perceive your action as a challenge. If you had trouble with the pitcher, avoid being where he will pass you on the way to the dugout. Don't chat with players. Answer their questions politely and let that be the end of it. Above all, don't coach.

One of the best techniques for handling confrontations is to let coaches finish what they are saying without interruption. Sometimes it can be comical to stand there and see how long it takes a coach to realize an umpire is not engaging him in argument. Soon the coach will wind down because he is carrying the entire discussion. By this time, he will have calmed down and you can explain the situation.

Unsporting Conduct

Be alert to unsporting comments from the dugouts and take immediate action to halt them. Frequent unsporting comments may cause you to lose control of the game. If you have trouble determining who is making the comments, inform the coach that you will remove someone in the area on the next occurrence.

Establishing Your Reputation

You build your reputation as an umpire as you go along. You obviously want to build a good reputation—one that reflects that you know the rules, know how to apply them, are fair and unbiased, are honest when you make a mistake and are in control. You want to build the reputation that you are solid and dependable, that players and coaches know they will get a fairly called game when you are in uniform.

Here we'll consider three ways you can build such a reputation—by being consistent, by using good judgment and by knowing how to handle your mistakes.

Being Consistent

Having a good game is great. Having two or three good games in a row is even better. What's best—and what will solidify your reputation—is when you are consistently good over many games.

One of the easiest ways to enhance your reputation is by being consistent in your ball and strike calls. As you develop your own strike zone (adjustable to batter height and stance), stay with it. Some umpires acquire reputations as low-ball or high-ball umpires. Some also become known for having a small strike zone or a large one. Managers, players and knowledgeable fans recognize and accept these discrepancies.

Most umpires don't purposely set out to earn any type of reputation in this manner; it just seems to develop. Having people think that way about your umpiring isn't harmful. What is harmful is being inconsistent with your strike zone—from game to game and especially within a game. When you maintain consistency with your strike zone, players and coaches know what to expect.

Remember, umpiring begins when you enter the park. From that point on, someone is watching you. On the other hand, when you leave the game, the only person you have to be satisfied with is yourself. Don't be overcritical of your performance. Things might seem bigger to you than they do to an outsider.

Finally, be consistent in your hustle. Hustle is synonymous with baseball. It's not just for players; it's for umpires, too. You have much to do with setting the tone of the game for everyone.

Using Good Judgment

As important as mechanics are in umpiring, school or league officials, managers, players and fans will not judge you on them. Most will consider you a good umpire if they believe that your judgment is good on ball or strike, safe or out, and fair or foul calls. Strive to exercise your best judgment and be consistent. Each complements the other.

If you want to advance in umpiring, what can you do after you have established your ability to exercise good judgment? You can increase your mastery of mechanics, improve your appearance and increase your understanding of the rules and their application to the game situations.

One of the most difficult tasks that you'll have is interpreting a rule to an upset manager. Stay calm and give a complete explanation of the rule and its application to the play. This clarification will go a long way toward gaining the manager's respect and toward building your reputation as a competent rules umpire. A good reputation does not come without considerable and consistent effort. Repeated reading and study of the *NFHS Baseball Rules Book* and *NFHS Baseball Case Book,* discussion of rules and plays with other umpires, attending rules meetings, viewing films and attending other presentations all contribute to your expertise here.

Handling Mistakes

To err is human. Umpires are human. You will miss some pitches and make some errors in judgment. Do your best to make as few errors as possible. When you boot a call or miss a pitch, do not resolve to even the call next time. Once called, that's it. It's finished. You cannot fix a bad call. A missed pitch or booted call is gone forever.

Evaluating Additional Issues

You should consider a handful of other issues in your mechanics as a plate umpire. We'll address those issues here.

Removing Your Mask

Remove your mask with your left hand. Never remove or hold your mask in your right hand because you need that hand free to signal calls. Some umpires seldom take the mask off, probably because they haven't learned to do it without having the cap come off with it. You'll have less trouble if you lift the bottom out from the chin, using the top of the mask as a hinge. Bring it straight out and up, clearing the visor. Tossing the mask aside is a part of the catcher's technique, but this practice is not permissible for umpires, nor is parking your mask on the top of your head.

Cleaning the Plate

To keep the plate clean, use a small broom—for two reasons. One, it can be placed in your shirt pocket, in your coat breast pocket or in the back pocket of your trousers without being too noticeable. Two, the plate surface area isn't very big; a small broom is more than sufficient.

When you start cleaning the plate, do so in a quick and professional manner and face the spectators (that is, with your back to the pitching mound) and the catcher's box. This stance looks better to the fans, and if your pants were to tear, only the infielders would see it.

Brush the plate during natural pauses in the game and between half innings. Stopping play to clean the plate when not necessary can disrupt the game and a team's momentum. If the batter or catcher requests that you clean the plate, however, do so promptly and willingly. Also, remember that when you're cleaning the plate, you have a good opportunity to communicate with the catcher.

Ball Supply

Rotate the baseball supply given to you at the beginning of the game. Don't try to save a newer ball for the darker innings. If it becomes too dark to play, stop the game (or have the lights turned on).

Be sure that you have a minimum of three unscuffed and untorn baseballs to start the game. You are responsible for approving them. Throw out any balls that become unplayable, being certain that you have at least two to finish the game. If the home team runs out of baseballs, check with the visiting team. If the visiting team is unable to furnish any balls, ask to see the home team's practice balls and select the best ones to complete the game.

Between Innings

Be productive between innings. In a game in which you are not having any trouble, walk down the foul line toward the team that is taking the field and encourage them to hustle out to their positions, being tactful as you do so. Don't nag but try to minimize delay. Then move back closer to the catcher's area, close enough to be able to supply another ball to the catcher should a warm-up pitch get past him.

Use the time the pitcher takes to throw his warm-up pitches for such tasks as getting the balls you need and inspecting them for playability. Try to relax during this time, perhaps going over in your mind your performance in the previous innings.

As you can see, the plate umpire has a myriad of duties and responsibilities. And while the duties of a field umpire are different, they are no less important. In the next chapter we'll explore field umpire mechanics.

CHAPTER 4

FIELD UMPIRE MECHANICS

As a field umpire (or base umpire, if more than one umpire is in the field) you'll have plenty of calls to make, although not as many as the plate umpire. Although your duties might be fewer than those of the plate umpire, they are just as important in carrying out a game that is safe and fair for both sides.

In this chapter, then, we'll look at the mechanics of being a field umpire—your positioning in the field, how to make calls and how to respond to specific plays.

Positioning

Your positioning on the field is the first step toward helping you in your field umpire duties. Here we'll look at a couple of issues related to positioning.

Initial Position on the Field

When the game is about to begin, station yourself by the foul line in foul territory about 10 feet behind the first baseman's playing position. Don't let the first baseman out of your sight. If he has to make a quick move, it shouldn't come as a surprise to you. Your peripheral vision should enable you to avoid interfering with or crowding a player. Use your head and eyes to keep from having to scurry out of the way of players.

Posture and Preparation

Exhibit proper posture on the field at all times. Don't fold your arms; this gives the wrong image. And don't cross your legs or slouch on one leg. Instead, relax your arms at your sides and place your feet far enough apart to be comfortable. This stance helps you concentrate on the game and sends the message that you're focused on the action—which you should be. Always keep your mind on the game. Don't let it wander to other subjects. If you do, it's only a matter of time until you're in trouble and trying to catch up on the game.

With the responsibility of having the final say on half swings, you must be ever alert at the time of the pitch. Don't respond to the first baseman's request on a half swing, however, just because he is closest and the easiest to hear. Wait until the plate umpire requests your decision by pointing toward you.

One simple move that you will find helpful is to step toward the batter at the time of the pitch. Timing is important. You'll get a feel for it. Make your stride about the time the pitcher releases the ball. If the batter doesn't hit the pitch, relax and return to your original position. If he hits the pitch, get into whatever position the play dictates. Doing this on each pitch keeps you alert, attentive and ready for any play. The movement also shows players and fans that you are interested and alert. This one step toward the batter is useful at every position you take on the infield.

Making Calls

Although you won't be making a call on every pitch, as you will when you are the plate umpire, you still have plenty of calls to make. Here we'll consider the types of calls you have to make and how to make them.

Out Call

The mechanics for calling an out are simple. The out call is a stand-up one and the same everywhere with only minor individual style variations.

Spread your feet so that you're comfortable, flex your knees and bend your body forward slightly at the hips. Keep your back straight. The position of your hands at the start of the out call is important; your hands should be down at your sides. This position gives you a starting point for the signal. Keep the fingers of your left hand lightly against your thigh during the entire out sign to ensure that you'll make your call with one arm. To make the call, bring your right hand up toward the side of your head (see figure 4.1). By using this technique, you won't give fans and players the impression that you started to give the safe sign and changed your mind.

Remember to wait until the play is completed. Don't be in a hurry to call it.

Suit your simultaneous oral call to the emphasis of the physical call and direct it to the offensive player, saying, "Out!" or, "You're out!"

FIGURE 4.1   Field umpire calling an out.

Safe Call

The safe call is just as important as the out call. Calling a player safe is simple. If you're moving, come to a halt as you begin the sign. With your feet shoulder-width apart or wider, raise your hands to shoulder height and fully extend them in front of your body. Then move your arms from in front of your body to each side in a continuous motion (see figure 4.2, a and b).

That's all there is to a routine safe sign. But if the play demands more emphasis or if you want to show your appreciation of a good play (a close play at first, a steal, a close pickoff play), bring your arms in from the extended position and re-extend them. You can repeat this a few times, depending on the amount of emphasis you wish to give. Another way of emphasizing the call is to take a couple of quick side steps, either with the arms extended or while making repeated safe signs.

Make your vocal call correspond in emphasis with that of your physical call. "You're safe!" or "Safe!" with proper emphasis usually does it.

You don't need to emphasize plays that are not close. Sometimes you make no call because there is no play on the runner. When a player hits a double, for example, you obviously don't give the safe sign as the runner rounds first.

You might find that you have a tendency to look down when you're making the safe call, thinking the action is over. Don't—you could miss other significant action. For example, the ball might squirt away from the fielder and the runner might try to advance, or another base runner might be subsequently caught in a rundown.

FIGURE 4.2 Field umpire calling safe (a and b).

You Make the (Close) Call

Baseball is a game of inches. Bang-bang plays at first base and fair or foul calls are just two of the close calls you'll make in the field. Some of the most-contested calls are steals of second base, pickoff plays at first base, rundown plays and force plays.

You should respond to plays like these by being in proper position, by getting a good look, by waiting until the play is completed and you're sure of the call, and then by clearly making the call. The closer the play, the more emphasis you want to give your call, both orally and through your signal.

Although a game often consists of a few hundred pitches and numerous plays in the field and at the plate, the one or two close plays are what people often remember. When you observe proper mechanics, you're placing yourself in position to make the call—no matter how close it is.

Timing of the Call

With the safe call and the out call, as with all calls, timing is of the essence. If your call is premature, the next action could render it wrong. Allowing too much time to elapse between the action and the call gives the appearance of uncertainty.

Style

Keep your style in perspective. Safe or out calls are to the field umpire what ball or strike calls are to the plate umpire. Just as the strike gestures of plate umpires must have the basic elements in common, so too must the basic elements of the safe and out signs of base umpires be similar. Those playing and watching the game need to get the message instantly without having to figure it out. If your safe and out signs are markedly different from those of other umpires, players and fans might misinterpret them.

Where then does individual umpire style come in? As in any endeavor in which style is not the sole end, style in umpiring comes most naturally through individual differences that appear as you seek to do your best. Using your whole body to communicate in the fashion and with the emphasis that the game situation demands will project your style. No one can justifiably accuse you of showboating if you use all the emphasis at your command to call a player safe or out when the play is crucial to the game.

Coverage

On all routine plays you will watch the batter-runner touch first and second bases and watch the runner on first touch second. The plate umpire will watch the runner touching and retouching third base. As noted in chapter 3, if you go out on a fly ball, the plate umpire should try to observe all runners.

Remember that your primary responsibility is the ball. If you do not see a runner miss a base, you can't make the call. But if you don't know whether a ball is caught or is fair or foul, it makes no difference if a runner misses a base.

Specific Plays

Besides those calls, you'll have calls to make in some other situations, including double-play situations, tag plays, and obstruction or interference situations.

Double-Play Situation

As a field umpire the call you'll likely be challenged on most often is the double play—specifically, the back end of it (the call at first base). When you use correct footwork, you'll be able to make the call at second and then get a good angle for the play at first. Be sure you stop before making the call at first. Being a few feet farther away but stationary is better than being a little closer to the bag but moving.

As the play develops, watch the infielder field the ball and make the throw to the pivot man to start the double play. Watch the throw for its accuracy and let the throw lead you to the play. Your judgment of the play involves these factors:

1. Seeing the pivot man's foot touch base.
2. Listening for the ball hitting the pivot man's glove.
3. Not turning your head too soon on the front end of the double play. If the pivot man drops the ball, judge whether he completed the force play and then dropped the ball while taking it out of his glove for the relay throw.
4. Picking up the relay throw to first while getting into position to make the call there.
5. Watching for the first baseman's foot to tag the base and listening for the ball to hit his mitt.
6. Being ready to ask for help from the plate umpire on a tag play when the pivot man's throw pulls the first baseman off the base.

Tag Play

The closer you can position yourself to a tag play, the better—but make sure that you don't station yourself so close that you hinder the players. Take a position at an angle where you can see the area between the base and the runner. (When taking your position, be sure that you are stationary. Ideally, you should have your hands on your knees and your head perfectly still.) A runner who is tagged while off the base is not out if the fielder fails to hold the ball. Also, watch for overslides—runners sometimes beat the throw but overslide or miss the base, so don't make your decision until the play is completed. A common error on these plays is ruling prematurely. Timing, a skill that you learn over the years, is paramount to good umpiring.

Obstruction and Interference

Any umpire who sees obstruction or interference can call it. Always signal a delayed dead ball or a dead ball, whichever the situation demands.

A ball becomes dead immediately when the batter interferes with the catcher's fielding or throwing (when the batter interferes with the catcher's throw, if an out doesn't result from the throw, the ball is dead immediately). A dead ball also occurs when the batter-runner runs outside the 3-foot running lane while the ball is being fielded or thrown to first base.

Some situations in which a delayed dead ball on obstruction or interference occur include obstruction of a batter or runner by a fielder, interference with the catcher who is attempting to throw by an umpire, or physical assistance given to a runner by a coach.

Because a dead ball or delayed dead ball call might create controversy, make sure that you use a proper signal when obstruction or interference occurs (see figure 4.3). Using the correct signal often precludes an argument and is evidence of your competency and control of the game. Although these calls are often contested, don't let this possibility affect your making the correct call. Use a loud voice and good animation.

In the last two chapters we've looked at the mechanics for plate umpires and field umpires. Now let's move on to crew mechanics—two-umpire, three-umpire and four-umpire crews. We'll explore two-umpire mechanics in the next chapter.

FIGURE 4.3 Field umpire calling an obstruction or interference for dead ball.

CHAPTER 5

TWO-UMPIRE MECHANICS

In chapters 3 and 4 you learned some of the basics of being a plate umpire and a field umpire. Now you'll delve into positioning, duties and responsibilities, and field mechanics and coverage for all situations that you will encounter as part of a two-umpire crew.

First, a few definitions are in order. For our purposes U1 is the plate umpire, U2 is the field umpire, R1 is the lead runner, and R2 and R3 are trail runners.

U1 begins each play, of course, behind home plate. U2 will be in one of three positions, depending on the runner situation:

- With no runners on base, U2 should use position A (see figure 5.1). Place both your feet in foul territory, about 10 feet behind the first baseman.

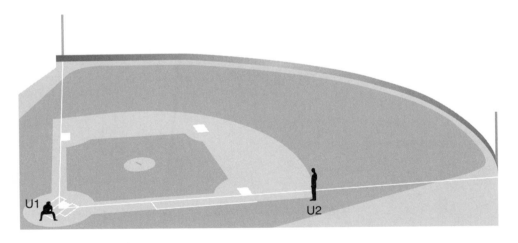

FIGURE 5.1   Position A for U2.

- With a runner on first base, use position B. Place yourself about half-way between the pitcher's mound and second base, on the first-base side of the infield (see figure 5.2). You should be more or less on a line extended from the plate through the edge of the mound, with your feet positioned parallel to the pitcher's plate so that you can move to cover a pickoff attempt at first or an attempted steal of second.

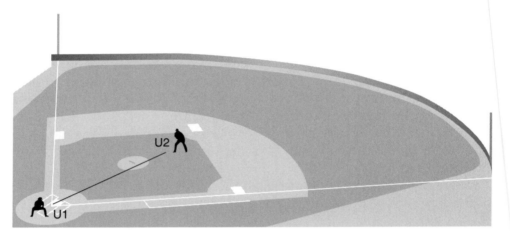

FIGURE 5.2   Position B for U2.

- With a runner as far as second base, use position C. Place yourself about halfway between the pitcher's mound and second base, on the third-base side of the infield (see figure 5.3). You should be more or less on a line extended from the plate to the edge of the mound, with your feet positioned parallel to the pitcher's plate so that you can move to cover an attempted pickoff or steal at any base.

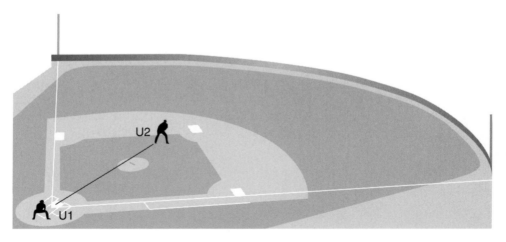

FIGURE 5.3   Position C for U2.

General Duties and Responsibilities

In this section we'll consider the general duties and responsibilities of the plate umpire and the field umpire. We'll look at the plate umpire first.

Plate Umpire

Your main responsibility as plate umpire, of course, is to call balls and strikes. But it extends far beyond that. Make sure you're always on your toes and hustling so that you can be in proper position to make your calls.

Beyond balls and strikes, here are your general responsibilities:

- *Batted balls.* Get your mask off and move on all batted balls. Throughout this chapter we'll tell you where you should move.
- *Batter-runner's position.* With a throw to first base from near home plate, observe the batter-runner's position in relation to the 3-foot running lane. If the batter-runner is not in the lane and interferes with the throw, call interference and call the batter-runner out.
- *Fair or foul rulings.* Rule on fair or foul situations from the plate to the left-field foul pole. If U2 is in position A, rule fair or foul on all batted balls that come to rest or are played on in front of first base. Rule fair or foul on all batted balls from the plate to the right-field foul pole if U2 is in position B or C. Be careful not to rule too soon.
- *Ground balls to the infield.* On ground balls to the infield, come inside the infield and be ready to move to cover plays that are your responsibility and to help your partner. Watch ground balls close to the line carefully to make the fair or foul call. With a runner at third, be careful not to go with the ball. Watch the play from the base line extended so that you can see the runner touch the plate.
- *Fly balls to the infield.* On fly balls to the infield, call catch or no catch on foul flies up to both bags and on fair flies to the left of second base or taken by the pitcher or catcher.
- *Fly balls to the outfield.* On fly balls to the outfield with U2 in position A, call catch or no catch on any fly ball that U2 does not go out on. You have the catch or no-catch responsibility on all fly balls hit to left field or on which the center fielder turns his back toward U2. You also have responsibility for balls hit to center field that move the center fielder to his right or left. If U2 is in the infield, call catch or no catch on all fly balls to left or right field in which the outfielder moves toward his respective foul line.
- *Tag-ups.* Watch the tag-up by any runner at third base or the tag-up by the lead runner in a situation involving multiple runners.

- *Plays at third or first.* Be prepared to move to third base if a play happens there on a batted ball. Be ready to move to first base to help your partner on a throw behind the runner or for a rundown, if possible.
- *Pop fouls.* On a pop foul to the catcher, move with the catcher while observing him and not the ball. Do not remove your mask until the catcher has tossed his mask. If the catch is near the screen, position yourself so that you will know if the ball touched the screen.

Field Umpire

You have a variety of duties as field umpire. As we noted in chapter 4, taking a step or two toward home plate with the pitch is helpful. This movement keeps you attentive and ready to move in any direction.

Like the plate umpire, you must hustle on every play to get in the right position to make the call. The following information will help you get in the right position and know what calls are yours to make.

- *Positioning.* With no runners, you will always be in position A; with a runner on only at first, you will always be in position B; with a runner as far as second base, you will always be in position C (see figures 5.1-5.3 on pages 51 and 52). This positioning is the same regardless of the number of outs.
- *Fair or foul calls.* In position A, call fair or foul on balls hit down the first-base line from the front edge of the bag to the foul pole, especially on balls bounding over the bag. Be alert to help U1 on a slow roller or bunt down the line when the catcher or batter-runner might block U1's view. If you see a batted ball contact the batter in the batter's box, call, "Dead ball!"
- *First play by an infielder.* This play is always your call, except at home plate. Let the ball take you into the play.
- *Catch or no-catch calls.* Make catch or no-catch calls on fly balls in these situations (remember not to cross the base paths when moving to make a call):
  - Call fly balls in the infield taken by the first or second baseman.
  - When in position A, go out to make a call on any difficult catch by the right fielder or the center fielder moving in any direction other than toward left field. Expect to go out on any fly ball to right or center that might involve a fair or foul decision, a catch below the waist (possible trap), a possible home run or a situation in which two fielders converge.

Getting the Angle

Without question, the biggest challenge of a two-umpire crew is getting the proper angle to call plays. How do you and your crewmate get the right angle? Through experience, anticipation (that is, considering the possibilities before a play happens), hustle and communication. The best umpires understand that angle is more important than distance; that is, you don't necessarily have to run a long way to get the best angle. You're more likely to get the play right if you have the proper angle as opposed to getting as close to the play as you can.

For example, with runners at first and second and none or one out, you should be positioned in the infield, about halfway between the pitcher's mound and second base, on the third-base side of the infield. On a ground ball that is fielded and thrown to second base for a force-out, watch to make sure that the infielder makes the force play. Let the infielder at second base lead you into the play. Most often the player will make the throw to first base to attempt a double play, but in certain situations the fielder might attempt to throw the runner out at third (if, for example, there's no chance to get the batter-runner at first and the runner at third has rounded the bag too far). Either way the play goes, you're ready to turn and make the call with the proper angle.

- Always go out on a close fair or foul call.
- On routine fly balls, come in and take a pivot, that is, move in closer to the infield and situate yourself near the player who will receive the ball. U1 will make the catch or no-catch ruling.
- When in position B or C, make the catch or no-catch ruling on fly balls to the outfield unless a fielder moving to a foul line attempts the catch. In this instance U1 has both the fair or foul call and the catch or no-catch ruling.
- *Tag-ups.* Line up the tag-up by a single runner, unless the runner is at third base. The home-plate umpire observes the tag-up at third. You'll also need to observe the tag-ups by following runners in a multiple-runner situation (U1 observes the lead runner).
- *Home plate and third base.* Move to cover home if U1 is at third and there are no following runners or to take a following runner into third if U1 has a play at the plate, as in a bases-loaded situation.

Field Mechanics and Coverage

In this section we'll cover all the situations you will face in a two-umpire crew. For each situation, we'll provide the mechanics and coverage for the plate umpire and the field umpire. These are the situations we'll cover:

- No runners on base
- Runner at first
- Runner at second
- Runner at third
- Runners at first and second
- Runners at second and third
- Runners at first and third
- Bases loaded

No Runners on Base

When there are no runners on base, the plate and field umpires have specific areas of coverage and positions for all plays that will occur in a game situation. The plate and field umpires should each be aware of their individual responsibilities when there are no runners on base.

Plate Umpire

As the plate umpire you have these duties with no runners on base:

- *All batted balls.* Move out on all batted balls and be ready to move to make a call on the batter-runner advancing to third base (see figure 5.4). You are responsible for the ground rules on an overthrow at first. In case of an overthrow, move toward foul territory with the path of the overthrown ball.
- *Fly balls.* You have a variety of duties on fly balls, depending on the situation and where the ball is hit:
  - If U2 has the catch or no-catch call on a fly ball (on the right side of the infield and down to the right-field foul pole), move to watch the batter-runner touch first base and be prepared to cover any attempted play on the batter-runner returning to first or to move to make a call at second base if U2 is held up by a ball down the line (see figure 5.5).
  - Call catch or no catch on all fly balls to the left side of the infield or fielded by the pitcher or catcher. Also make this call on any foul fly balls fielded by the first baseman between the plate and the first-base bag.

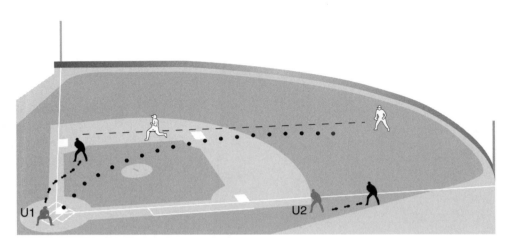

FIGURE 5.4   U1 moving to make a call on the batter-runner advancing to third.

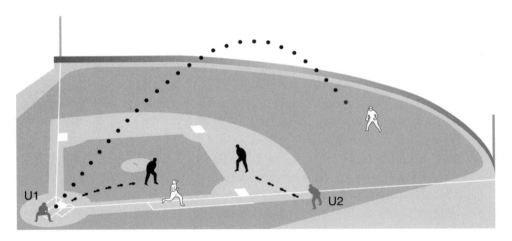

FIGURE 5.5   U1 moving into position on a fly ball to right field.

- Call catch or no catch on all fly balls to left field (see figure 5.6) and on which the center fielder moves to his right (left field). On routine fly balls to center field or right field, call catch or no catch if U2 comes in to take a pivot. Make the call orally to assist U2, who is watching the batter-runner touch first base.

- *Fair or foul calls.* Call fair or foul on all batted balls down the third-base line to the foul pole in left field and on all batted balls that are played on or come to rest between home and the front edge of first base. Follow bunted balls down the line.

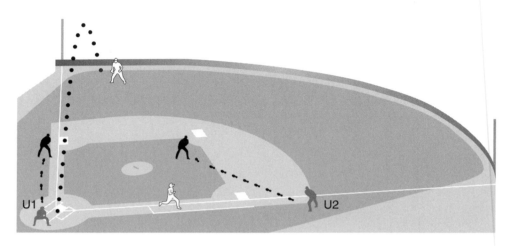

FIGURE 5.6   U1 moving into position on a fly ball to left field.

Field Umpire

With no runners on base, you should be in position A (see page 51) when you are the field umpire. Here are the mechanics of your coverage in this situation:

- *Calls at first base.* Move to make all calls at first base on plays in the infield. To get a good angle, take three or four quick, hard steps toward the player fielding the ball and then set and let his throw turn you to the bag.
- *Base hits.* On base hits, come into the infield, pivot to watch the batter-runner touch first base and be ready to move to second base if he should attempt to advance (see figure 5.7).

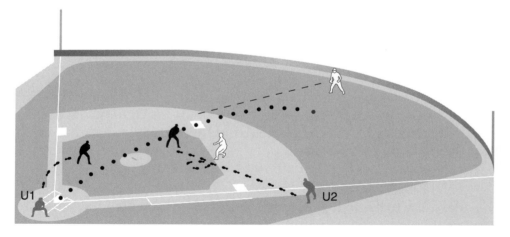

FIGURE 5.7   U2 moving into position to make a call on a base hit to right field with runner advancing to second.

- *Extra-base hits.* On an extra-base hit, take the batter-runner only as far as second base; U1 has him at third. Be alert for the runner returning to second or advancing home on an overthrow at third. Cover the plate for U1 in the latter case (see figure 5.8).

- *Fair or foul and catch or no-catch calls.* Go out on fair or foul situations, possible traps, potential home runs or when the center fielder and left fielder are converging and may possibly collide. You have catch or no-catch jurisdiction on balls hit to the right fielder (see figure 5.9) and fly balls to the center fielder that move him in, out toward the fence or toward right field. Be ready to return to take the play at the plate because U1 has the bases behind you. Be sure to review fly-ball coverage in your pregame discussion with your partner. You must communicate that you are going out on a fly ball so that your partner does not fail to take the batter-runner around the infield. If you are going to take the catch, immediately call out, "I've got the ball!" to alert your partner to watch the batter-runner.

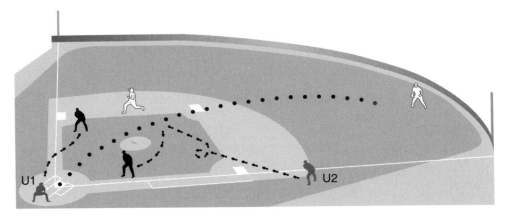

FIGURE 5.8   U2 moving into position on an extra-base hit to the outfield.

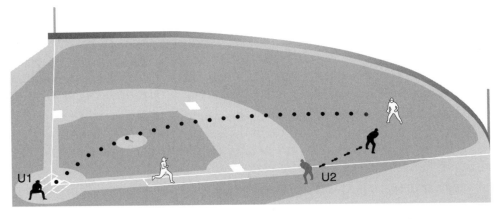

FIGURE 5.9   U2 moving into position on a ball hit to the right fielder.

Runner at First Base

When there is a runner at first base and no other runners on, the plate and field umpires have specific areas of coverage and positions for all plays that will occur in a game situation. The plate and field umpires should each be aware of their individual responsibilities when there is a runner at first base and no other runners on. The starting positions are as shown in figure 5.10.

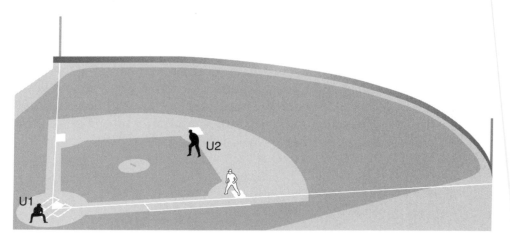

FIGURE 5.10   U1 and U2 starting positions with a runner at first base.

Plate Umpire

As plate umpire, you have these responsibilities:

- *All batted balls.* Move out on all batted balls and be ready to move to cover a play at third base. The second play in the infield at third base belongs to you. If R1 advances to third on a base hit, the play at third belongs to you unless the ball was hit down the right-field line. In that case U2 would take R1 to third (see figure 5.11). Go back to the plate on an overthrow at third.

- *All plays in the infield.* Watch all plays in the infield so that you can help if your partner asks. Watch for interference by the retired runner at second base and then look quickly to see if the first baseman keeps his foot on the bag. Offer help only if your partner asks.

- *Catch or no-catch calls.* Call catch or no catch on all fly balls fielded by the pitcher or catcher and on balls down either line. Also make this call on all foul fly balls and on any fly ball to the outfield in which the fielder moves toward a foul line to make the play.

- *Fair or foul calls.* Call fair or foul on all balls down both lines to the foul poles. Follow bunted balls down the line.

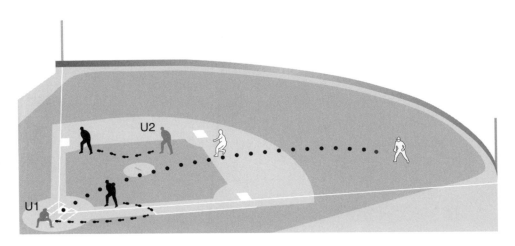

FIGURE 5.11   U1's coverage on a ball hit down the right-field line, with U2 covering third.

Field Umpire

With a runner at first base and no other runners on, you should be in position B (page 60). These are your responsibilities as field umpire:

- *Pickoff attempts.* Be alert for pickoff attempts at first, by either the pitcher or catcher (see figure 5.12, a and b). Watch for possible balks as well. A quick step or two toward the plate before turning on a pickoff will improve your angle at first.

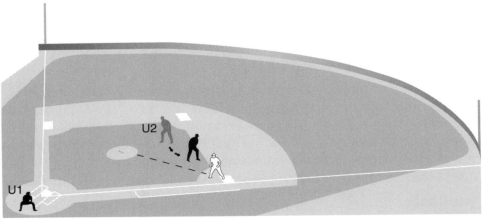

a   *(continued)*

FIGURE 5.12   U2's movements on a pickoff attempt by the pitcher at first *(a)* and an overthrow at first *(b).*

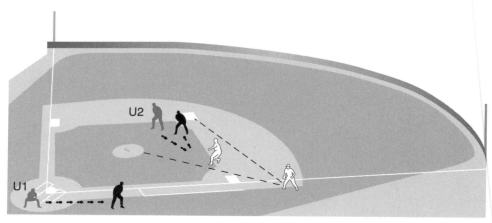

b

FIGURE 5.12   *(continued)*

- *Attempted steals.* On an attempted steal of second, step back toward second and let the throw turn you to the play (see figure 5.13a).
- *Base hits.* On base hits, watch the runner from first touch second and the batter-runner touch first and any succeeding bases (see figure 5.13b).
- *First plays in the infield.* Call the first play in the infield. On double plays, after seeing the force at second, turn and move to see the play at first base.
- *Catch or no-catch calls.* Call catch or no catch on fly balls fielded in the middle of the infield and on fly balls to the outfield between the left and right fielders.
- *Checked swings.* Be ready to help your partner on checked swings, despite the poor angle you will have.

Runner at Second Base

When there is a runner at second base and there are no other runners on, the plate and field umpires have specific areas of coverage and positions for all plays that will occur in a game situation. The plate and field umpires should each be aware of their individual responsibilities when there is a runner at second base and there are no other runners on. With a runner at second base only, the starting positions are as shown in figure 5.14.

Plate Umpire

As plate umpire, these are your coverage responsibilities:

- *Fair or foul calls.* Rule fair or foul on ground balls from home plate to the foul pole down both lines. Follow bunted balls down the line but be alert for plays at home plate.

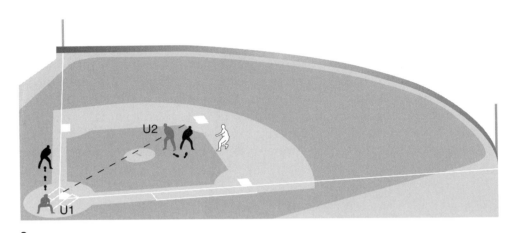

a

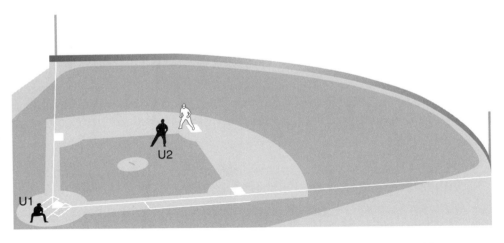

b

FIGURE 5.13   U2 stepping back into position to make a call of an attempted steal of second base *(a)* and covering a base hit *(b)*.

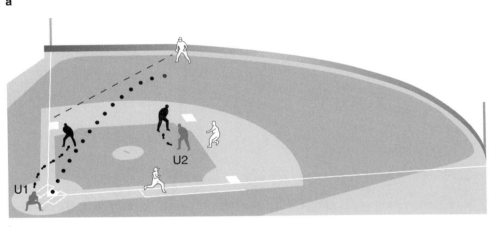

FIGURE 5.14   U1 and U2 starting positions with a runner at second base.

- *Base hits.* On a base hit, observe R1's touch of third base and be ready to cover a play on R1 advancing to home plate.
- *Runner trapped between second and third.* On a ball hit in the infield in which R1 is trapped between second and third, watch the batter-runner touch first then move to third to help your partner if the rundown continues. U2 should be flexible to rule on R1 retreating back to second or R2 advancing to second (see figure 5.15). Chances are good that the batter-runner will try to advance to second during a prolonged rundown.

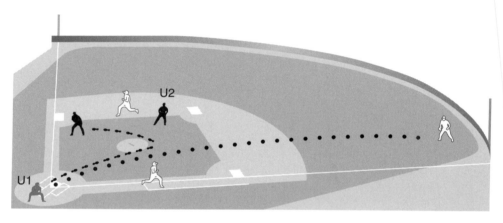

FIGURE 5.15   U1's coverage in a rundown situation.

- *Catch or no-catch calls.* Call catch or no catch on all fly balls fielded by the pitcher or catcher and on balls down either line. Also make this call on all foul fly balls and on any fly balls to the outfield in which the fielder moves toward his respective foul line.
- *Safe or out calls.* Call safe or out on R1 advancing after a caught fly ball, except on a fly down the right-field line. When you are moving into position, watch for the pitcher moving to third to back up the play. Be prepared to call the play at third base if it is the second play in the infield (see figure 5.16).

Field Umpire

With a runner at second and no other runners on base, you should be in position C (see figure 5.14) as field umpire. These are your coverage responsibilities:

- *Pickoff attempts.* Watch for possible pickoff attempts at second by either the pitcher or the catcher (see figure 5.17).
- *Attempted steals.* Be alert for attempted steals of third base. A quick step toward the plate before turning to move to the base will improve your angle on the steal play (see figure 5.18).

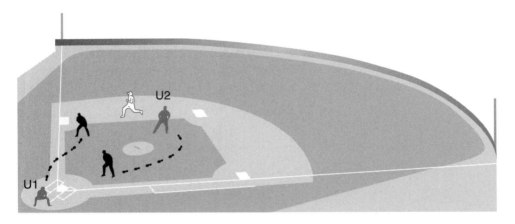

FIGURE 5.16 U1's coverage of third base.

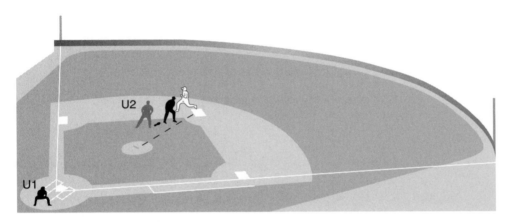

FIGURE 5.17 U2 moving to cover a pickoff attempt.

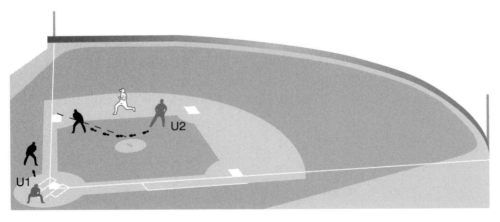

FIGURE 5.18 U2 getting in position to cover an attempted steal of third base.

- *Ground balls to the infield.* On ground balls in the infield, watch the ball as it is fielded and let the throw take you to the play. Remember that the play is not always to first base, so don't anticipate. If the play is to first, move toward the bag, get set, make the call and then take a step or two toward the bag after making the call (see figure 5.19).

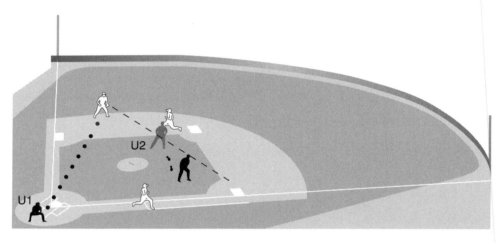

FIGURE 5.19   U2's positioning on a ground ball and subsequent throw to first base.

- *Catch or no-catch calls.* Call catch or no catch on fly balls fielded in the middle of the infield and on fly balls to the outfield between the left and right fielders.
- *Caught fly balls.* Move to observe the tag-up by R1 attempting to advance to third on a fly ball hit to the outfield. U1 has the play at third, and you will have any subsequent play at the plate (see figure 5.20a). If U1 has gone down the right-field line to rule fair or foul, or catch or no catch, you must take R1 into third base (see figure 5.20b).
- *Throws to second.* On routine fly balls or plays in the infield in which R1 is not advancing to third, be alert for throws to second base attempting to catch R1 off the bag.
- *Base hits.* On base hits, watch the batter-runner touch first and second.

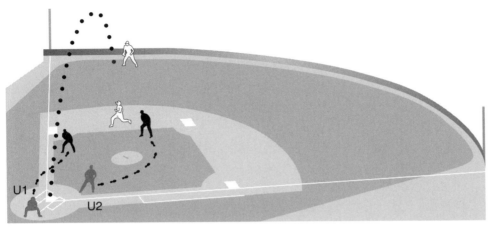

a

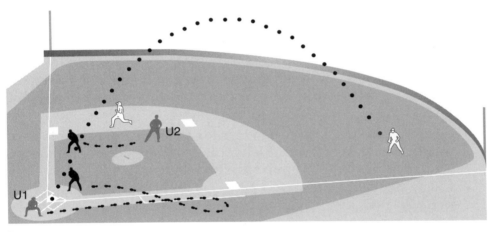

b

FIGURE 5.20   U2's coverage on a caught fly ball to the left *(a)* and right *(b)* with a runner advancing to third.

Runner at Third Base

When there is a lone runner at third base, the plate and field umpires have specific areas of coverage and positions for all plays that will occur in a game situation. The plate and field umpires should each be aware of their individual responsibilities when there is a lone runner at third base. Starting positions are as shown in figure 5.21.

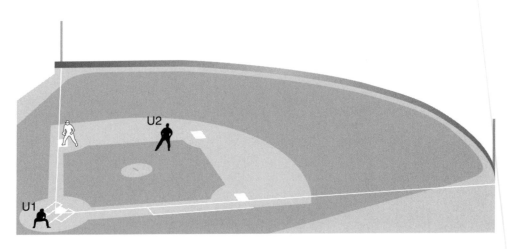

FIGURE 5.21   U1 and U2 starting positions with a runner at third base.

Plate Umpire

Your coverage as plate umpire is as follows:

- *Focus on the plate.* Your movement is limited because of a potential play at the plate. You will make all calls if R1 advances to home plate.
- *Squeeze plays and steals.* Be alert for possible squeeze plays or attempted steals of home. Make sure that the pitcher's delivery is legal. Be sure to call the pitch first and then the play.
- *Fair or foul calls.* Make fair or foul calls on all balls down both lines to the foul poles.
- *Catch or no-catch calls.* Call catch or no catch on all fly balls fielded by the pitcher or catcher or down either line, on all foul fly balls and on any fly balls to the outfield in which the fielder moves toward his respective foul line.
- *Sacrifice flies.* On fly balls on which R1 may tag up and score, move to line up the tag.
- *Base hits.* On base hits, watch R1 touch home plate and then be ready to move to cover third if necessary.

Field Umpire

As field umpire you should be in position C with a runner at third base. As with a runner at second, you need to be alert for pickoff attempts, watch ground balls to the infield (not anticipating that the throw will go to first but letting the throw turn you to the play) and watch the batter-runner touch first and second bases on a hit. In addition, you'll make the catch or no-catch call on fly balls fielded in the middle of the infield and on fly balls to the outfield between the left and right fielders. Stay in; do not cross the base paths to go out to make a call.

Runners at First and Second

When there are runners at first and second, the plate and field umpires have specific areas of coverage and positions for all plays that will occur in a game situation. The plate and field umpires should each be aware of their individual responsibilities when there are runners at first and second. Starting positions are as shown in figure 5.22.

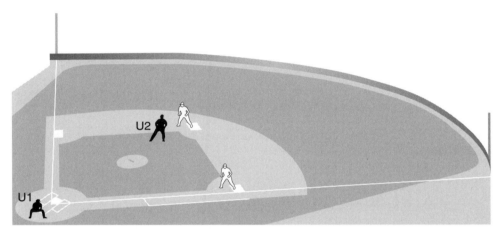

FIGURE 5.22   U1 and U2 starting positions with runners at first and second base.

Plate Umpire

Your responsibilities as plate umpire include the following:

- *Infield-fly rule.* Be aware of the infield-fly situation with less than two outs; signal your partner.
- *Fair or foul calls.* Call fair or foul down both lines to the foul poles.
- *Catch or no-catch calls.* Call catch or no catch on all fly balls fielded by the pitcher or catcher or down either line, on all foul fly balls, and on any fly balls in the outfield on which the left or right fielder moves toward his respective foul line. Observe the tag-up by R1 at second base on any fly ball hit to the outfield.
- *Ground balls to the infield.* On ground balls in the infield, move to watch the slide of an advancing runner on a double-play attempt; also watch the touch of third base by the advancing R1. Move to be able to make a call at third if the first play in the infield is at first or

second; any succeeding play at third is yours (see figure 5.23). Any potential play at the plate following a bobbled ball or a double-play attempt would be yours as well.

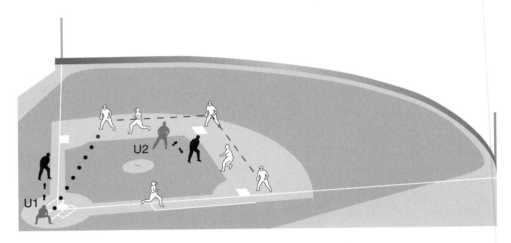

FIGURE 5.23   U1 moving into position for a possible call at third on an attempted double play.

- *Advances on fly balls.* Move to observe the tag by R1 at second base on a fly ball to the outfield. Be prepared to take the play at third base if R1 advances after a fly ball. On a ball hit down the right-field line, U2 will take the tag and R1 into third base. If R1 does not tag or if the fielder drops the ball, stay home and be prepared for a play at the plate.
- *Base hits.* On base hits, observe R1's touch of third base and move to make the call on R1's advance to the plate. Also be ready to move to third for a play on R2.
- *Plays at third base.* Be prepared to call a play at third base if it is the second play in the infield, unless R1 is advancing to home.

Field Umpire
With runners at first and second, you should be in position C (page 69) as field umpire. Your duties include the following:

- *Infield-fly rule.* Be aware of the infield-fly situation with less than two outs; signal your partner.
- *Catch or no-catch calls.* Call catch or no catch on fly balls fielded in the middle of the infield and on fly balls to the outfield between the left and right fielders. Be alert for line drives that might become double plays.
- *First plays in the infield.* Call the first play in the infield. On double plays, after seeing the force-out, turn and move to get in position for

the back end of the play (see figure 5.24a). Don't anticipate what the play might be.

- *Fly balls to the outfield.* On fly balls to the outfield, observe the tag by R2 at first base and by R1 at second base if U1 has coverage on a ball hit down the right-field line. Take the call on R2 advancing to second base or R1 returning to second. Take R1 advancing to third if U1 has a fair or foul call down the right-field line on a fly ball or if U1 stays at home because the fly ball is not caught.

- *Base hits.* On base hits, watch R2 touch second base and then turn to pick up the batter-runner touching first (see figure 5.24b). Make all calls at second or first and be prepared to take following runners into third if U1 has a call at home.

a

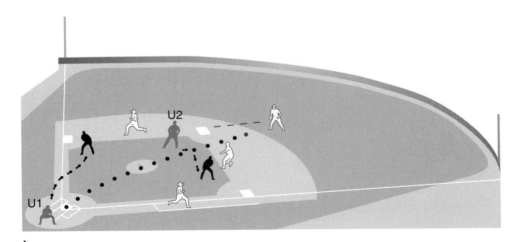

b

FIGURE 5.24   U2's areas of coverage on a ball hit to the infield *(a)* and on a base hit *(b)*.

Runners at Second and Third

When there are runners at second and third, the plate and field umpires have specific areas of coverage and positions for all plays that will occur in a game situation. The plate and field umpires should each be aware of their individual responsibilities when there are runners at second and third.

Plate Umpire

With runners at second and third, your movement as a plate umpire will be limited because of a potential play at the plate. You'll make all calls on R1's advance to home (see figure 5.25, a and b), and you'll also be responsible for the following:

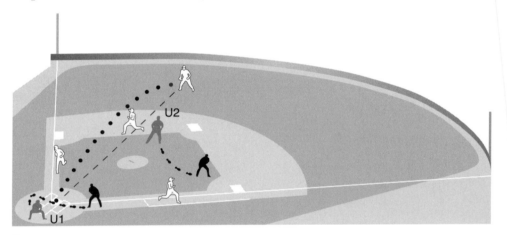

a

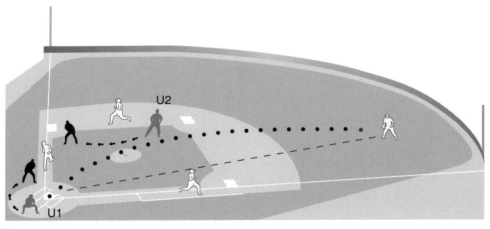

b

FIGURE 5.25   U1 making the catch or no-catch call *(a)* and moving into position for a call at home *(b)*.

- *Attempted steals and squeeze plays.* Be alert for a possible steal of home or a squeeze play. Make sure that the pitcher's delivery is legal. Be sure to call the pitch first and then the play.
- *Fair or foul calls.* Call fair or foul down both lines to the foul poles.
- *Catch or no-catch calls.* Call catch or no catch on all fly balls fielded by the pitcher or catcher or down either line, on all foul fly balls and on any fly balls in the outfield on which the left or right fielder moves toward his respective foul line.
- *Tag-ups.* Move to line up the tag by R1 at third on any fly ball to the outfield. Make calls at home plate from the baseline extended.
- *Time-play situations.* With two outs, be alert for a time-play situation involving R2 and the batter-runner. Signal your partner. Watch the play on R2 and listen for your partner's call to determine if R1 scores before the third out.
- *Ground balls to the infield.* On a ground ball in the infield with the first play being made at first, move up the third-base line in foul ground (see figure 5.26). Watch R1 touch home, and get into position to make a call on R2 at third.
- *Base hits.* On a base hit, move up the third-base line in foul ground as you do on a ground ball in the infield. Watch R1 touch home plate and then get in position either to move to third or to retreat to home for a play on R2.

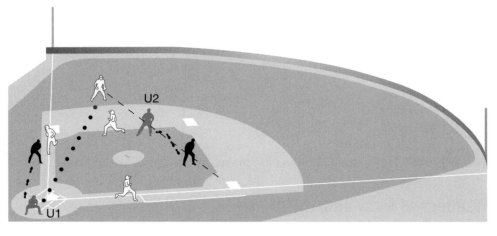

FIGURE 5.26   U1 moving up the third-base line on a ground ball in the infield.

Field Umpire

As field umpire you should be in position C with runners at second and third. Be prepared to make these calls:

- *Pickoff attempts.* Be alert for possible pickoff attempts at second or third by the pitcher or catcher. Be sure that the pitcher's move is legal.
- *Catch or no-catch calls.* Call catch or no catch on fly balls fielded in the middle of the infield and on fly balls to the outfield between the left and right fielders.
- *Tag-ups.* On fly balls to the outfield, move to line up the tag-up by R2 at third base (see figure 5.27).
- *Time-play situations.* With two outs, be alert for a time-play situation involving R2 and the batter-runner. Signal your partner. Make the out call on the batter-runner in a loud voice so that your partner can hear it.
- *Base hits.* On base hits, watch the batter-runner touch first base and be prepared to take him either into second base or back to first base.

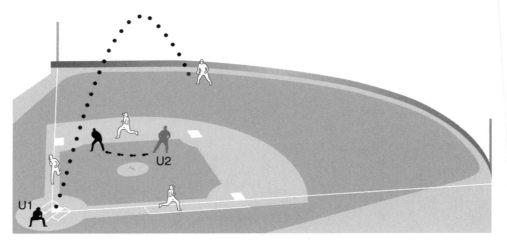

FIGURE 5.27   U2 getting into position to line up the tag by R2 at third.

Runners at First and Third

When there are runners at first and third, the plate and field umpires have specific areas of coverage and positions for all plays that will occur in a game situation. The plate and field umpires should each be aware of their individual responsibilities when there are runners at first and third.

Plate Umpire

With runners at first and third, the starting positions are as shown in figure 5.28. Your duties as plate umpire include the following:

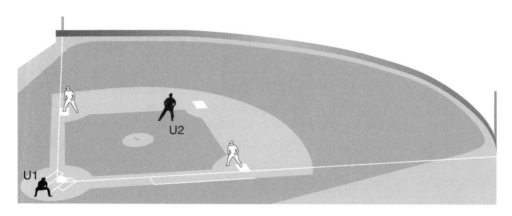

FIGURE 5.28   U1 and U2 starting positions with runners at first and third.

- *Calls at home.* Be alert for a possible steal of home or a double steal. A squeeze is a possibility as well.
- *Fair or foul calls.* Call fair or foul down both lines to the foul poles.
- *Catch or no-catch calls.* Call catch or no catch on all fly balls fielded by the pitcher or catcher or down either line, on all foul fly balls, and on any fly balls to the outfield on which the left or right fielder moves toward his respective foul line.
- *Lead runner first.* On any play situation, move to watch R1 touch home plate and then cover other plays. On ground balls in the infield, your second responsibility is to watch the play at second for interference on an attempted double play. If the first play on a ground ball is on R1 at home, remember that the play is not a force.
- *Fly balls to the outfield.* On fly balls to the outfield, move to line up the tag-up by R1 at third base and then move back to the plate.
- *Base hits.* On base hits, move toward third in foul ground, ready to cover third on a play there or to retreat to the plate if R2 attempts to score on the hit (see figure 5.29).

FIGURE 5.29   U1 ready to cover third and retreat to home if necessary.

Field Umpire

As field umpire you will be in position C (see figure 5.28) with runners at first and third. You will have the following duties:

- *Pickoff attempts.* Be alert for pickoff attempts by the pitcher or catcher at first or third. Make sure that the pitcher's move is legal on the feint to third followed by a throw back to first.
- *Delayed double steals.* Especially with two outs, watch for the delayed double steal rundown play. Be sure to make a loud and clear call on the putout because of the time-play potential.
- *First plays.* Make any call on the first play by an infielder except at the plate. Be alert for line drives that might become double plays. On ground-ball double plays, watch the force-out and then move and turn to get into position for the call on the back end of the play.
- *Catch or no-catch calls.* Call catch or no catch on fly balls fielded in the middle of the infield and on fly balls to the outfield between the left and right fielders.
- *Base hits.* On base hits, watch R2 touch second and then look to see the batter-runner touch first. Remain aware of the positions of the runners and your partner, because R2 might try to return to second or become caught in a rundown between second and third, in which case the play at second is yours. If the batter-runner attempts to reach second, the play at second also is yours. Obviously, communication will be important in avoiding double calls, or worse, no calls.

Bases Loaded

When the bases are loaded, the plate and field umpires have specific areas of coverage and positions for all plays that will occur in a game situation. The plate and field umpires should each be aware of their individual responsibilities when the bases are loaded. Starting positions for this situation are shown in figure 5.30.

Plate Umpire

As plate umpire you'll be responsible for the following plays and situations:

- *Plays at the plate.* Be alert for a steal, passed ball or squeeze play. Call the pitch first and then the play. Hold your position on all balls in play to make calls on any runner advancing to home plate. Be careful not to get too close to the play, on either a force-out or a tag, because you don't want to be taken out on the play. First watch R1 touch the plate and then look to cover other plays, such as interference on an attempted double play.

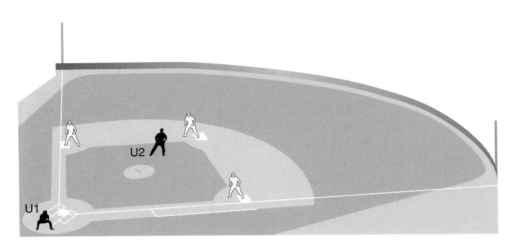

FIGURE 5.30   U1 and U2 starting positions with the bases loaded.

- *Fair or foul calls.* Call fair or foul on balls down both lines to the foul poles.
- *Catch or no-catch calls.* Call catch or no catch on all fly balls fielded by the pitcher or catcher or down either line, on all foul fly balls and on any fly balls in the outfield on which the left or right fielder moves toward his respective foul line.
- *Tag-ups.* Move away from the plate to line up the touch by R1 at third base on fly balls to the outfield. If it is clear that no play will occur at the plate, move up the third-base line in foul ground while watching R1 score in case of a play at third base. Let your partner know that you have third covered.
- *Time plays and infield flies.* Be alert for possible time-play situations with two outs or infield-fly situations with less than two outs. Signal your partner in either situation.

Field Umpire
As a field umpire with the bases loaded, you should be in position C. Watch and be prepared to call these plays:

- *Attempted pickoffs.* Be alert for any potential pickoffs. Make sure that the pitcher's move is legal.
- *Catch or no-catch calls.* Call catch or no catch on fly balls fielded in the middle of the infield and on fly balls to the outfield in between the left and right fielders.
- *First-play calls.* Make the call on the first play on a ground ball hit in the infield at any base except home.
- *Tag-ups.* Move to line up the tag by R2 at second base on fly balls to the outfield (see figure 5.31); look back at first to get some hint

FIGURE 5.31   U2 getting into position to line up the tag-up by R2.

about R3's tag at first. If the throw after the catch goes to the plate, be ready to move to any base to make a call on an advancing or returning runner.

- *Base hits.* On base hits, watch R3 touch second, look to see the batter-runner touch first and be ready to go wherever you are needed to make a call. Generally, calls at first and second are yours; third and home belong to your partner. Communicate! In this situation, the two of you are outnumbered by possible play situations, so effective communication with your partner is vital.

- *Time-play situations and infield flies.* Be alert to potential time-play situations with two outs and infield-fly situations with less than two outs; signal your partner.

You'll probably use two-umpire mechanics quite often. But you might be scheduled as part of a three-umpire crew at times as well. The next chapter examines the mechanics of three-umpire crews.

CHAPTER 6

THREE-UMPIRE MECHANICS

In a three-umpire crew the mechanics are split up a bit more than they are in a two-umpire crew. As in the previous chapter, we'll explore the positions, responsibilities and coverage for all situations for a three-umpire crew, with U1 being plate umpire, U2 being first-base umpire and U3 being third-base umpire.

U1 starts behind the plate on all plays. U2 and U3 begin either near their respective corner base or on their side of second base. Depending on the situation, they take one of these four basic positions.

- *Position A for U2.* Stand with both feet in foul territory, about 10 feet behind the first baseman (see figure 6.1a).
- *Position B for U2.* Stand about halfway between the pitcher's mound and second base, on the first-base side of the infield (see figure 6.1b). Position your feet parallel to the pitcher's plate so that you can move to cover a pickoff attempt at first or an attempted steal of second.
- *Position C for U3.* Stand about halfway between the pitcher's mound and second base, on the third-base side of the infield (see figure 6.1c). Position your feet parallel to the pitcher's plate so that you can move to cover any attempted pickoff or steal at any base.
- *Position D for U3.* Stand with both feet in foul territory, about 10 feet behind the third baseman (see figure 6.1d).

All positions remain unchanged regardless of the number of outs. Position D mirrors position A, except that position D is on the third-base side of the diamond. When you're in position A or D, move up closer to the bag if a runner is on first base (position A) or third base (position D). This location will give you an angle on a pickoff attempt and help you line up the pitcher's foot crossing over the back edge of the pitcher's plate. You will be in position to see if the pitcher's pickoff move is legal or not.

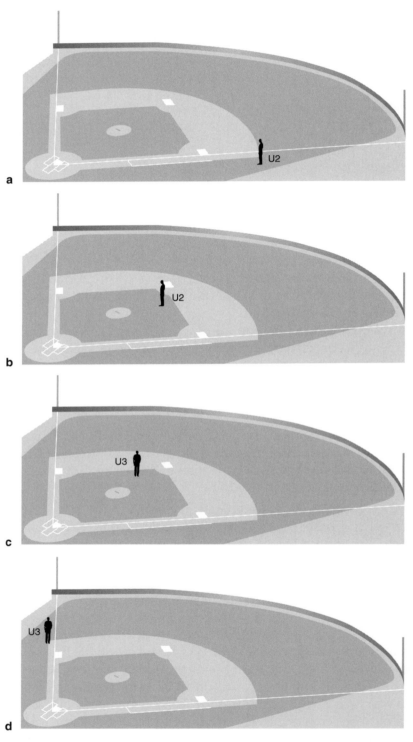

FIGURE 6.1   Positions A, B, C and D *(a-d)*.

General Duties and Responsibilities

Here we'll explore the general duties and responsibilities of U1, U2 and U3. First we'll look at the umpire behind the plate.

U1 Responsibilities

Here are your main duties as plate umpire:

- *Balls and strikes.* You, of course, call these.
- *Checked swings.* Appeal checked swings on right-handed batters to U2 and on left-handed batters to U3.
- *Fair or foul calls.* Rule fair or foul on any batted ball that is played on or comes to rest in front of the front edge of the base down the first-base line with U2 in position A and down the third-base line with U3 in position D (see figure 6.2). If either U2 or U3 is in the infield, rule fair or foul all the way to the foul pole on the exposed side.

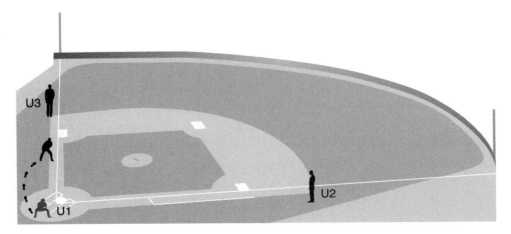

FIGURE 6.2   U1 going down the third-base line to make the fair or foul call.

- *Catch or no-catch calls.* Rule catch or no catch on all foul fly balls behind home plate and up to the first- and third-base bags, on any fly balls taken by the catcher, and on fly balls or line drives to the pitcher.
- *Batted balls.* When the ball is hit, move out from behind the plate to be ready to go to cover a base or line up a fly ball when you are responsible for observing a tag-up. Watch every play as if it were yours to call, both because your partners may appeal to you for help

and because as umpire-in-chief you may be required to decide on play situations involving rules.

- *Infield-fly rule and time plays.* Signal your partners in an infield-fly situation and when a two-out time play is possible.

U2 Responsibilities

When you're in position A, remember to move one or two steps with the pitch so that when the ball is hit, you are ready to move to cover any play for which you are responsible. Your primary responsibilities as U2 are as follows:

- *Calls at first.* Make calls at first base on plays in the infield.
- *Fair or foul calls.* Rule fair or foul on ground balls down the first-base line from the front of the bag to the foul pole, especially on balls bounding over the bag, and on fly balls from the bag to the foul pole if in position A. Call, "Dead ball!" on all foul balls that hit the batter in the batter's box.
- *Catch or no-catch calls.* Rule catch or no catch on fly balls and line drives in the infield taken by the first or second baseman.
- *Infield fly and time plays.* Signal your partners in an infield-fly situation and when a two-out time play is possible.
- *Checked swings.* Respond only if U1 asks. U1 should appeal to you on right-handers, even if you are in position B.

U3 Responsibilities

When you're in position D, remember to move one or two steps with the pitch so that when the ball is hit you are ready to move to cover any play for which you are responsible. Note that if either U2 or U3 goes out to the outfield to make a call, coverage reverts to the two-umpire system. The umpire who goes out to the outfield stays out. Your responsibilities as U3 include the following:

- *Ground balls and base hits.* Move toward position C (see page 80) on ground balls and base hits to cover plays at second base.
- *Fair or foul calls.* Rule fair or foul on ground balls down the third-base line from the front of the bag to the foul pole, especially on balls bounding over the bag, and on fly balls from the bag to the foul pole if in position D. Call, "Dead ball!" on all foul balls that hit the batter in the batter's box.
- *Catch or no-catch calls.* Rule catch or no catch on fly balls and line drives in the infield handled by the shortstop or third baseman.

- *Infield fly and time plays.* Signal your partners in an infield-fly situation and when a two-out time play is possible.
- *Interference calls.* Rule on possible interference by the runner at second base on an attempted double play.
- *Checked swings.* Respond only if U1 asks for help. U1 should appeal to you on left-handers, even if you are in position C.

Field Mechanics and Coverage

In this section we'll cover all the situations you will face in a three-umpire crew. For each situation we'll provide the mechanics and coverage for U1, U2 and U3. We'll cover these situations:

- No runners on base
- Runner at first
- Runner at second
- Runner at third
- Runners at first and second
- Runners at second and third
- Runners at first and third
- Bases loaded

No Runners on Base

In this section we'll outline the coverage for U1, U2 and U3 with no runners on base. Figure 6.3 shows the starting positions for all three umpires.

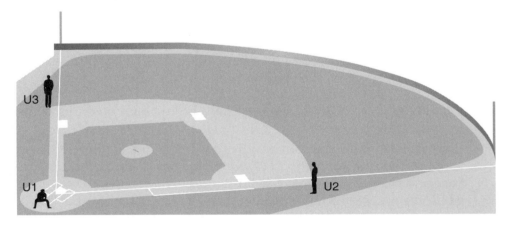

FIGURE 6.3   U1, U2 and U3 starting positions with no runners on base.

U1 Coverage

The following list notes the coverage for U1 in various situations.

- *All batted balls.* Move out on all batted balls; be ready to move to cover the batter-runner advancing to third base.
- *If U2 goes out to the outfield.* If U2 goes out, move to watch the batter-runner touch first base and be alert to cover any attempted play on the batter-runner returning to first (see figure 6.4). U1 has first base and will retreat to home. U3 has plays at second and third.

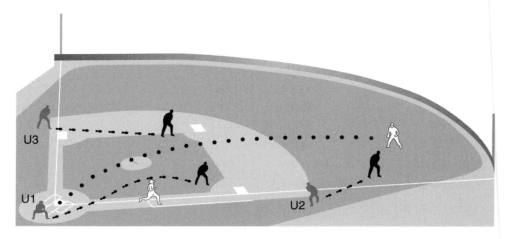

FIGURE 6.4   U1 moving toward first base if U2 goes out to the outfield.

- *Catch or no-catch calls.* Call catch or no catch on all fair fly balls taken by the catcher, on fly balls and line drives taken by the pitcher, and on all foul fly balls between home and the first- or third-base bag.
- *Fair or foul calls.* Call fair or foul up to the front edge of the first- and third-base bags. Follow bunted balls down the line.

U2 Coverage

With no runners on base you will be in position A as U2 (page 83). Here are your main responsibilities with no runners on base:

- *Calls at first base.* Move to make all calls at first base on plays in the infield.
- *Batter-runner.* If U3 goes out on a fly ball or is pinned at third base on a fair or foul call, come in, pivot, watch the batter-runner touch first base and be ready either to take him into second base or to cover on a ball thrown behind him as he returns to first. (Realize that you'll get no help from U1, who has the batter-runner if he attempts to advance to third.) Be ready to go home on an overthrow of third.

- *Base hits.* On a base hit, come in, pivot, watch the batter-runner touch first base and be ready to cover on a ball thrown behind him as he returns to first (see figure 6.5). On an extra-base hit, come in, pivot, watch the batter-runner touch first base and then be alert to cover home if U1 has gone to third base.

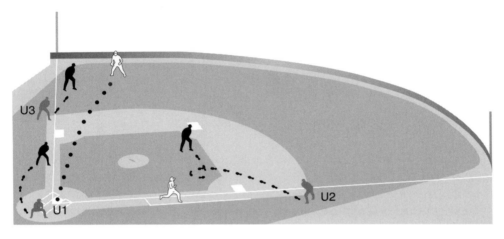

FIGURE 6.5   U2 coming in to pivot on a base hit.

- *Catch or no-catch calls.* Call catch or no catch on fly balls to center field in which the center fielder moves to his left or straight back, on any fly balls to right field, on all fly balls or line drives taken by the first or second baseman, and on foul fly balls past the first-base bag. Go out on potential problems, such as when two fielders are going after a fly ball near a foul line.
- *Fair or foul calls.* Call fair or foul on ground balls past the front edge of the first-base bag or bounding over the bag and on all fly balls past the first-base bag.

U3 Coverage

With no runners on base you will be in position D (see page 83) as U3. Here are your main responsibilities with no runners on base:

- *Ground balls and base hits.* Move toward position C on all ground balls or base hits to make calls on any play at second base (see figure 6.6). Don't return to third; U1 has the runner advancing to third base.
- *If U2 goes to the outfield.* If U2 goes out, go toward position C. If U1 takes the play at third, release the batter-runner at second base and move to cover any subsequent play at home. U1 has first and will retreat to home. U3 has plays at second and third.

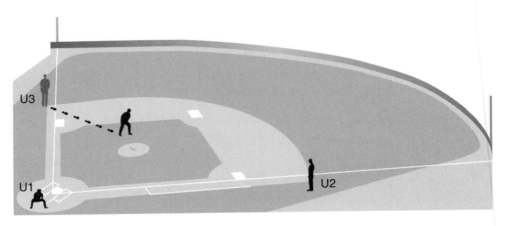

FIGURE 6.6   U3 going to position C on a ground ball or base hit.

- *Catch or no-catch calls.* Call catch or no catch on fly balls to center field in which the center fielder moves to his right or comes straight in, on any fly balls to left field, on all fly balls or line drives taken by the shortstop or third baseman, and on foul fly balls past the third-base bag. Go out on potential problems.
- *Fair or foul calls.* Call fair or foul on ground balls past the front edge of the third-base bag or bounding over the bag and on all fly balls past the third-base bag. If you are pinned at third on a fair or foul call, stay in position there.

Runner at First Base

Here we'll delineate the coverage of U1, U2 and U3 with a runner at first base and no other runners on. Figure 6.7 shows the starting positions for all three umpires.

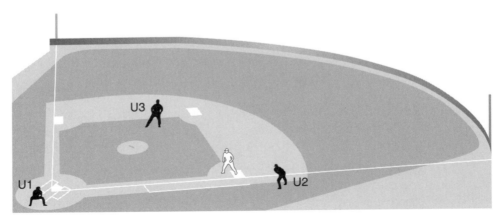

FIGURE 6.7   U1, U2 and U3 starting positions with a runner at first base.

U1 Coverage

As the umpire behind the plate, make sure that you move out on all batted balls and be ready to move to cover a play at third base. Watch all plays in the infield so that you can help your partners if asked. In addition, you are responsible for these calls:

- *Catch or no-catch calls.* Call catch or no catch on fair fly balls taken by the pitcher or catcher, on foul fly balls between home and the first- or third-base bag, and on fly balls down the third-base line in which the third baseman moves toward the third-base foul line.
- *Fair or foul calls.* Call fair or foul up to the front edge of the first-base bag and all the way to the foul pole down the third-base line. Follow bunted balls down either line.
- *If U2 goes to the outfield.* If U2 goes out on a fly ball, watch the tag of R1 at first base and the touch of the batter-runner at first.

U2 Coverage

You have the following coverage responsibilities with a runner on first base:

- *Attempted pickoffs.* With a runner on first your position will change slightly, although you are still in position A. To be able to make a call on an attempted pickoff, you should be in foul territory, 6 to 8 feet behind first base. Position yourself to get an angle on a pickoff. You should be able to look through the runner, the bag and the first baseman toward the pitcher. Remember to watch for a balk on a pickoff attempt. Signal safe or out on a pickoff only if a tag occurs.
- *Calls at first base.* Move to make all calls at first base on plays in the infield.
- *Batter-runner.* Watch the batter-runner touch first base on a base hit. Be ready to release the batter-runner and move to cover home plate if U1 goes to cover third base.
- *Rundowns.* Make the call on R1 returning to first base on a rundown, using outside position (see figure 6.8).
- *Fair or foul calls.* Call fair or foul on ground balls past the front edge of the first-base bag. Move to call fair or foul on fly balls past first base.
- *Catch or no-catch calls.* Call catch or no catch on fly balls in which the right fielder goes back or moves toward the right-field foul line, on all fly balls taken by the first or second baseman, and on all foul fly balls past the first-base bag.
- *Tag-ups.* Move to line up the touch and tag-up at first base on all fly balls if you're not responsible for the catch or no-catch call and on routine fly balls to right field.

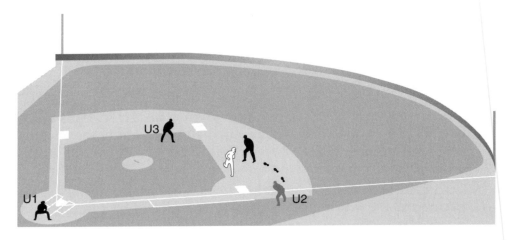

FIGURE 6.8   U2 using outside position in a rundown situation.

U3 Coverage

As U3 you'll be in position C with a runner on first base (see figure 6.7 on page 86). These are your main coverage responsibilities:

- *Attempted steals.* Turn with the catcher's throw to make the call on an attempted steal of second base.
- *If U2 goes out.* Move to cover both the batter-runner and R1 if U2 goes out for any reason (see figure 6.9).
- *Second-base calls.* Make all calls on plays at second base. Make the call on R1 advancing to second base on a rundown, using inside position (see figure 6.10).

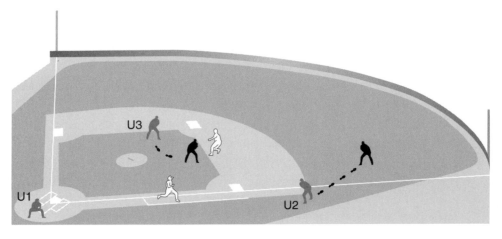

FIGURE 6.9   U3 covering the batter-runner and R1 as U2 goes out to the outfield.

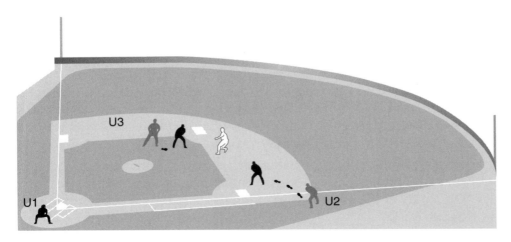

FIGURE 6.10   U3 making the call on R1 advancing to second base on a rundown.

- *Interference calls.* Be ready to call interference or illegal slides at second base on double plays.
- *Catch or no-catch calls.* Call catch or no catch on fly balls between left field and right field and on fair fly balls taken by the shortstop or third baseman (unless those are fair or foul calls, in which case the call is U1's). Do not leave the infield.

Runner at Second Base

Figure 6.11 shows the starting positions for all three umpires. Here are the coverage responsibilities for U1, U2 and U3.

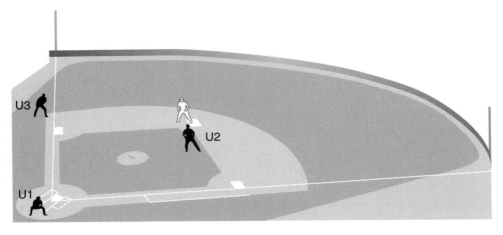

FIGURE 6.11   U1, U2 and U3 starting positions with a runner at second base.

U1 Coverage

U1 has various coverage responsibilities, depending on the play and the situation:

- *Fair or foul calls.* Rule fair or foul on ground balls from home plate to the front edge of the third-base bag and all the way to the foul pole down the first-base line. Follow bunted balls down either line but be alert for a possible play situation at home.
- *All batted balls.* When the ball is hit, move out from behind the plate; on a base hit, be ready to make a call on R1 advancing to home plate. On a play at the plate, set up along the first-base line extended (see figure 6.12).

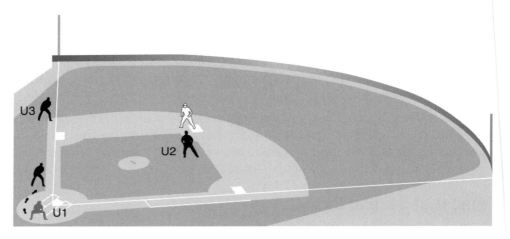

FIGURE 6.12   U1 setting up for a play at the plate.

- *If U3 goes out.* If U3 goes out for any reason, watch R1 touch third base and be in position to move to make a call on R1 returning to third base or advancing to home plate (see figure 6.13). On an extra-base hit, move up to make the call on the batter-runner advancing to third base.
- *Ground balls to the infield.* On a ground ball in the infield, watch the batter-runner touch first base if R1 has been caught in a rundown between second and third.
- *Catch or no-catch calls.* Call catch or no catch on fair fly balls taken by the pitcher or catcher, on fly balls to the outfield in which the right fielder moves toward the right-field foul line, and on all foul fly balls between home plate and the first- or third-base bag and down the right-field foul line.
- *Calls at home.* Make all calls on runners advancing to home plate.

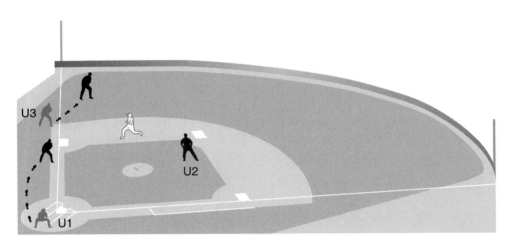

FIGURE 6.13   U1 moving to make the call on the batter-runner advancing to third base.

U2 Coverage

As U2 you will be in position B (see figure 6.11 on page 89) with a runner on second. Here are your main coverage responsibilities:

- *Calls at first base.* Move to make all calls on the batter-runner at first base.
- *Calls at second base.* Make all calls on R1 at second base. Be alert for R1 being caught between second and third on a ground ball.
- *Catch or no-catch calls.* Call catch or no catch on fly balls and line drives to the outfield between left field and right field and on fly balls taken by the first or second baseman (unless those are fair or four calls). Line up the tag-up of R1 advancing from second after a catch.
- *If U3 goes out.* If U3 goes out for any reason, coverage reverts to that used in the two-umpire system.

U3 Coverage

As U3 you will be in position D (see figure 6.11 on page 89) with a runner on second. These are your main coverage responsibilities:

- *Calls at third base.* Move to make all calls at third base on plays in the infield and on R1 advancing to third base after tagging up on a fly ball.
- *Catch or no-catch calls.* Call catch or no catch on fly balls in which the left fielder moves toward the left-field foul line or comes straight in, on all fly balls taken by the shortstop or third baseman, and on all foul fly balls past the third-base bag. Go out on fly balls in which the left fielder goes straight back.

- *Fair or foul calls.* Call fair or foul on ground balls past the front edge of the third-base bag, on balls bounding over the bag and on all fly balls past the third-base bag.

Runner at Third Base

Following are coverage responsibilities for all three umpires when a runner is on third base and no other runners are on. Figure 6.14 shows the starting positions for all three umpires.

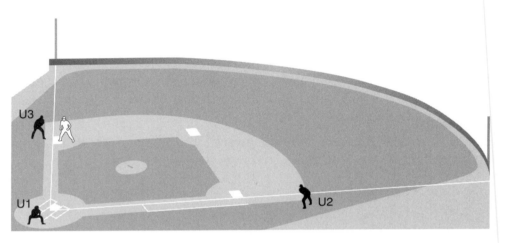

FIGURE 6.14   U1, U2 and U3 starting positions with a runner on third.

U1 Coverage

Your movement as U1 will be limited because of a potential play at the plate. Make sure that the pitcher's delivery is legal and be sure to call the pitch first and then the play. Here are your responsibilities:

- *Plays at the plate.* You will make all calls on R1 advancing to home plate. Be alert for an attempted steal of home, squeeze play or passed ball.
- *Tag-ups.* Move to line up the tag-up of R1 at third base if U3 goes out for any reason or if the left fielder makes the play by coming in or moving toward the left-field foul line.
- *Catch or no-catch calls.* Call catch or no catch on fair fly balls taken by the pitcher or catcher and on all foul fly balls from home plate to the first- and third-base bags.
- *Fair or foul calls.* Call fair or foul on ground balls from home plate to the front edge of the first-base or third-base bag.

U2 Coverage

As U2 you will be in position A with a runner on third and no other runners on (page 92). Your responsibilities include the following:

- *Calls at first base.* Move to make all calls at first base on plays in the infield.
- *If U3 goes out.* If U3 goes out on a fly ball or is pinned at third base on a fair or foul call, come in, pivot, watch the batter-runner touch first base, and be ready either to take him into second base or to cover on a ball thrown behind him as he returns to first (see figure 6.15). You won't get help from U1, who has a potential play at the plate.

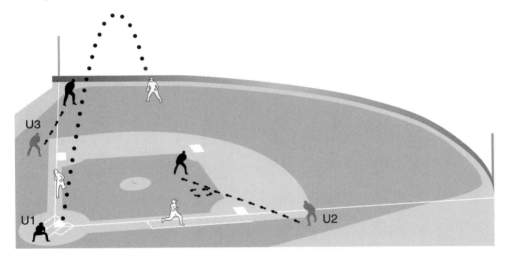

FIGURE 6.15   U2 watching first and getting into position to take the batter-runner to second.

- *Base hits.* On a base hit, come in, pivot and watch the batter-runner touch first base. On an extra-base hit, come in, pivot, watch the batter-runner touch first base and be ready to cover home if U1 has gone to cover third base. (Release the batter-runner when he reaches second base.)
- *Catch or no-catch calls.* Call catch or no catch on fly balls to center field in which the center fielder moves either to his left or straight back, on any fly balls to right field, on any fly balls taken by the first or second baseman, and on foul fly balls past the first-base bag.
- *Fair or foul calls.* Call fair or foul on ground balls past the front edge of the first-base bag, on balls bounding over the bag and on all fly balls past the first-base bag.

U3 Coverage

As U3 you should be in a slightly adjusted position D to begin play with a runner at third and no other runners on. Your feet should be in foul territory, 6 to 8 feet behind the third baseman (see figure 6.16). As always, be alert to help on checked swings by left-handed batters if U1 asks for your assistance. Make sure that R1 doesn't block your vision as you observe the swing.

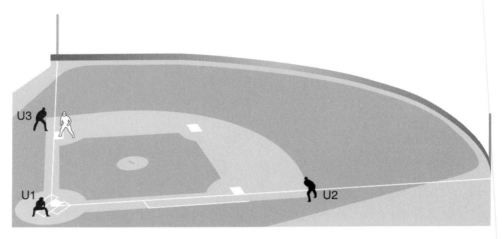

FIGURE 6.16   Adjusted position D for U3 with a runner on third.

Here are your essential duties:

- *Pickoff plays.* Move to get an angle on a pickoff if necessary. Signal safe or out on a pickoff only when the fielder attempts a tag. Hold your position for fair or foul calls if no pickoff attempt occurs.
- *Tag-ups.* Move to line up R1's tag-up at third base on fly balls fielded by the right fielder or center fielder (see figure 6.17). On any fly ball hit to the left fielder, move out to rule fair or foul, or catch or no catch; U1 will take the tag-up of R1.
- *Rundowns.* Make the call on R1 returning to third base on a rundown.
- *Calls at second base.* On base hits, move toward position C and take all calls at second base.
- *Catch or no-catch calls.* Call catch or no catch on fly balls to left field or center field, on any fly balls taken by the shortstop or third baseman, and on all foul fly balls past the third-base bag.
- *Fair or foul calls.* Call fair or foul on ground balls past the front edge of the third-base bag, on balls bounding over the bag and on all foul fly balls past the third-base bag.

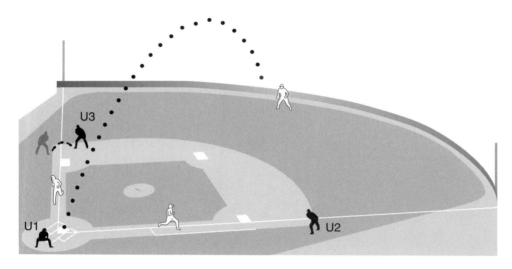

FIGURE 6.17 U3 moving to line up the runner's tag-up on a fly ball to center.

Runners at First and Second

With runners at first and second, umpires take the starting positions shown in figure 6.18.

FIGURE 6.18 U1, U2 and U3 starting positions with runners at first and second.

U1 Coverage

U1 has the following coverage responsibilities with runners at first and second:

- *All batted balls.* Move out on all batted balls. Be in position to watch the touch of third base by R1 advancing from second base on a base hit. Be ready to retreat to cover a play on R1 at home plate.

- *Calls at third base.* Move to third base to make a call on R1 advancing to third after tagging up on a caught fly ball (see figure 6.19). Be alert for the pitcher going to back up a play at third base. Hold your position at third on an overthrow; U2 will cover home.

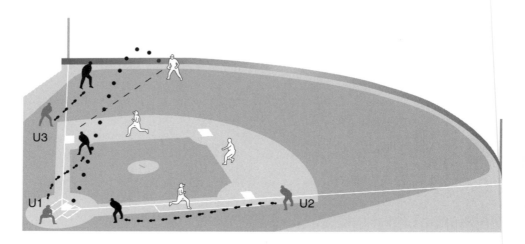

FIGURE 6.19   U1 going to cover an attempted advance to third by R1 after a caught fly ball.

- *Catch or no-catch calls.* Call catch or no catch on fly balls in which the left fielder moves toward the left-field foul line, on all foul fly balls down the third-base line, and on any fly balls taken by the pitcher or catcher.
- *Fair or foul calls.* Call fair or foul up to the front edge of the first-base bag and all the way to the foul pole down the third-base line. Follow bunted balls down either line.

U2 Coverage

As U2 you will be in position A with runners at first and second (see figure 6.18). Here are your main coverage duties:

- *Plays at first base.* Make all calls on plays at first base, including the back end of double plays.
- *Pickoff attempts.* Position yourself to get an angle on a pickoff play at first base. Be alert for a possible balk. Signal safe or out only if the fielder makes a tag.
- *Base hits.* On a base hit, watch the batter-runner touch first base and be ready to move to cover home if U1 goes to cover a play at third base.

- *Catch or no-catch calls.* Call catch or no catch on fly balls in which the right fielder goes back or moves toward the right-field foul line and on any fly balls taken by the first or second baseman. Move to line up the tag-up by R2 at first base on fly balls if you aren't responsible for the catch or no-catch call (see figure 6.20).

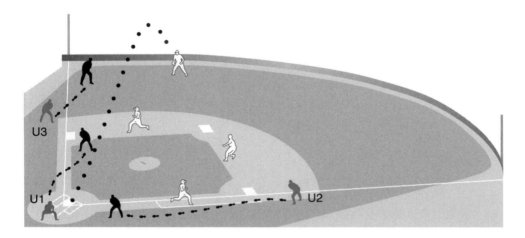

FIGURE 6.20   U2 moving to line up the tag-up by R2 on a fly ball to deep left-center field.

- *Fair or foul calls.* Be ready to make fair or foul calls on balls hit down the first-base line.
- *Time plays and infield-fly situations.* Signal time plays to U1 with two outs and signal infield-fly situations with less than two outs.

U3 Coverage

As U3 you should be in position C with runners on first and second (see figure 6.18 on page 95). Here are your essential responsibilities:

- *Pickoff plays and steals.* Be alert for a pickoff play at second base or an attempted steal of third base. On a steal attempt, be careful not to commit to third too early—the throw on a double steal might be to second base.
- *Calls at second base.* Call all plays at second base. Watch for the runner interfering when breaking up a double-play attempt.
- *Calls at third base.* Call a play at third base if it is the first play in the infield or if R2 or the batter-runner advances to third base.
- *Tag-ups.* On fly balls to the outfield, line up the tag-up by the runner at second base attempting to advance to third base. Be alert for R2

attempting to advance to second on a throw. Move to take tag-ups at both second and first if U2 goes out on a fly ball.

- *Catch or no-catch calls.* Call catch or no catch on fly balls between left field and right field and on fly balls taken by the third baseman or shortstop if they aren't fair or foul calls.
- *Time plays and infield-fly situations.* Signal a time play to U1 with two outs and signal an infield fly with less than two outs.

Runners at First and Third

With runners at first and third, umpires take the starting positions shown in figure 6.21.

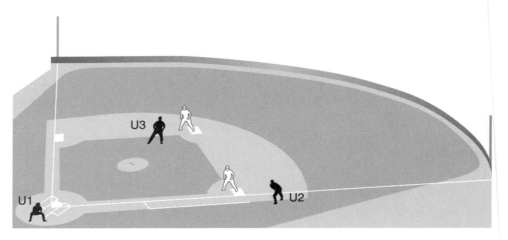

FIGURE 6.21   U1, U2 and U3 starting positions with runners at first and third.

U1 Coverage

U1 has these coverage responsibilities with runners at first and third:

- *Calls at home.* Make the call on R1 advancing home. Be alert for a steal, passed ball or squeeze attempt. Be sure to call the pitch first and then the play on the runner.
- *Tag-ups.* Line up the tag-up by R1 at third base on a fly ball to the outfield.
- *Catch or no-catch calls.* Call catch or no catch on fly balls on which the left fielder moves toward the left-field foul line, on all fly balls taken by the pitcher or catcher, and on all foul fly balls down the third-base line.
- *Base hits.* On any base hit, watch R1 touch home and move to cover a play on R2 or on the batter-runner advancing to third.

- *Fair or foul calls.* Call fair or foul to the front of the first-base bag and to the foul pole down third-base line. Make these calls from the base line extended to maintain position for a potential call on R1 advancing to home.

U2 Coverage

As U2 you will be in a slightly modified position A (page 98) with runners at first and third. Here are your essential duties:

- *Pickoff plays.* Position yourself to call a pickoff attempt at first base. Be alert for a balk.
- *Tag-ups.* Move to line up the tag-up by R2 at first base on a fly ball. Also be prepared to make a call on R2 returning to first.
- *Plays at the plate.* Watch the touch of first base by the batter-runner. Be prepared to move to the plate for a possible play if U1 goes to third to make a call on the advancing R2.
- *Catch or no-catch calls.* Call catch or no catch on fly balls in which the right fielder goes back or moves toward the right-field foul line, on any fly balls taken by the first or second baseman, and on all foul fly balls past first base.
- *Fair or foul calls.* Call fair or foul on balls past the front of the first-base bag.

U3 Coverage

As U3 you will be in position C (page 98) with runners on first and third, ready to make these calls:

- *Attempted steals.* Be alert for possible steal attempts at second base. Let the catcher's throw turn you into the play.
- *Calls at second base.* Make all calls at second base. Watch for interference by R2 attempting to break up a double play.
- *Catch or no-catch calls.* Call catch or no catch on fly balls between left field and right field and on any fly balls taken by the shortstop or third baseman if they aren't fair or foul calls.
- *Tag-ups.* If U2 goes out, move to line up the tag-up by R2 at first and the touch of first by the batter-runner. Be prepared to make a call on the batter-runner advancing to second base or returning to first base.
- *Calls at third base.* Be ready to make a call on R1 returning to third base after a caught fly ball.

Runners at Second and Third

When runners are at second and third, umpires should be in the starting positions shown in figure 6.22.

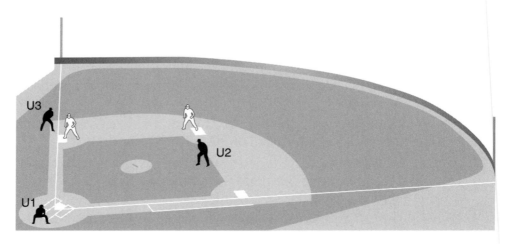

FIGURE 6.22   U1, U2 and U3 starting positions with runners at second and third.

U1 Coverage

Coverage responsibilities for U1 with runners at second and third are as follows:

- *Plays at the plate.* Call all plays on runners advancing to home plate. Be alert for possible steals, passed balls and squeeze plays. Be sure to call the pitch first and then the play on the advancing R1.
- *Tag-ups.* Move to line up the tag-up by R1 attempting to score on a fly ball to left field.
- *Catch or no-catch calls.* Call catch or no catch on fly balls in which the right fielder moves toward the right-field foul line, on any fly balls taken by the pitcher or catcher, and on all foul fly balls past the first-base bag.
- *Fair or foul calls.* Call fair or foul to the front of the third-base bag and to the foul pole down the first-base line. Make the call from the base line extended to maintain your position to make a call on a runner advancing home.

U2 Coverage

As U2 you should be in position B with runners at second and third, ready to make these calls:

- *Pickoff plays.* Be alert for pickoff plays at second base.

- *Calls at first and second.* Make all calls at first and second bases. Move on a base hit to watch the batter-runner touch first base and to be in position to make a call on his advance to second base or return to first.
- *Catch or no-catch calls.* Call catch or no catch on all fly balls from left field to right field and on any fly balls taken by the first or second baseman if they are not fair or foul calls.
- *Tag-ups.* Move to line up the tag-up by R2 at second base on a fly ball. Be ready to make a call on R2 advancing to third base if U3 goes out on a fly ball.
- *Time plays.* Signal a time play to U1 with two outs.

U3 Coverage
As U3 you should be in a slightly modified position D (page 100) when runners are at second and third. Here are your main responsibilities in this situation:

- *Pickoff attempts.* Be alert for pickoff attempts at third base by either the pitcher or the catcher.
- *Calls at third.* Make all calls on plays at third base.
- *Tag-ups.* Move to line up the tag-up by R1 at third base on a fly ball to center or right field.
- *Catch or no-catch calls.* Call catch or no catch on fly balls in which the left fielder moves toward the left-field foul line, on any fly balls taken by the shortstop or third baseman, and on all foul fly balls past the third-base bag.
- *Fair or foul calls.* Call fair or foul on balls past the front edge of the third-base bag.

Bases Loaded
With the bases loaded, the three umpires should be in the starting positions shown in figure 6.23.

U1 Coverage
Coverage responsibilities for U1 with the bases loaded are as follows:

- *Plays at the plate.* Make calls on all plays at home. Hold your position on balls in play in the infield or outfield to be ready to make a call on runners advancing to home. Be alert for steals, passed balls and squeeze plays. Be sure to call the pitch first and then the play on the runner.

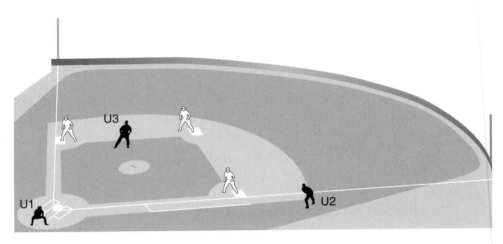

FIGURE 6.23   U1, U2 and U3 starting positions with the bases loaded.

- *Tag-ups.* Move to line up the tag-up by R1 at third base on fly balls.
- *Catch or no-catch calls.* Call catch or no catch on all fly balls taken by the pitcher or catcher, on all fly balls to left field in which the left fielder moves toward the left-field foul line, on all foul fly balls between home plate and the first- or third-base bag, and on all foul fly balls past the third-base bag.
- *Fair or foul calls.* Call fair or foul on batted balls up to the front edge of the first-base bag and all the way to the foul pole down the third-base line.

U2 Coverage

When you are U2, you should be in position A with the bases loaded, ready to make these calls:

- *Pickoff plays.* Position yourself to call pickoff plays at first base. Be alert to call balks as well.
- *Calls at first.* Make the call on all plays at first base.
- *Base hits.* On base hits, come in and pivot, watch the batter-runner touch first base and be ready to make the call at second base if U3 goes to cover third base.
- *Catch or no-catch calls.* Call catch or no catch on fly balls directly to right field or in which the right fielder moves toward the right-field foul line. Also make these calls on all foul fly balls past the first-base bag.
- *Tag-ups.* Move to line up the tag-up by R3 on a fly ball if you're not responsible for the catch or no-catch call.

- *Fair or foul calls.* Call fair or foul on batted balls past the front edge of the first-base bag.
- *Time plays and infield-fly situations.* Signal U1 for a time play with two outs and for an infield fly with less than two outs.

U3 Coverage

You should be in position C (page 102) with the bases loaded when you are U3. Here are your main responsibilities in this situation:

- *Pickoff attempts.* Be alert for possible pickoff attempts at second or third base by the pitcher or the catcher.
- *Force plays.* Make all calls on force plays at second and third bases. Watch for interference by a runner attempting to break up a double play.
- *Calls at third base.* Make the call on R1 returning to third base and on R2 and any following runners advancing or retreating to third after a base hit.
- *Tag-ups.* Move to line up the tag-up by R2 on fly balls.
- *Catch or no-catch calls.* Call catch or no catch on all fly balls between left field and right field and on all fly balls taken by the shortstop or third baseman if they aren't fair or foul calls.
- *Time plays and infield-fly situations.* Signal U1 for a time play with two outs and for an infield fly with less than two outs.

Probably most of your time will be spent in two-umpire or three-umpire crews. But on occasion—typically in state tournaments or other large competitions—you might find yourself having the luxury of being part of a four-umpire crew. But it's no luxury if you don't know how to operate within such a crew. In the next chapter we guide you through four-umpire mechanics.

CHAPTER 7

FOUR-UMPIRE MECHANICS

Although you might not often have occasion to work in a four-umpire crew—such crews are typically reserved for state playoff games—at times you may find yourself in that situation. This chapter will help prepare you for your duties in a four-umpire crew.

In a four-umpire crew, U1 is the plate umpire, U2 is at first, U3 is at second and U4 is at third. The positions of the first- and third-base umpires are generally the same as those described in earlier chapters (U2 in position A, U4 in position D). U3, the second-base umpire, has three positions:

- *Position E.* Stand in the outfield behind second base and on the side from which the batter hits (see figure 7.1).

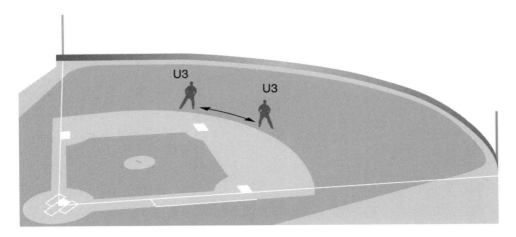

FIGURE 7.1   U3 in position E.

- *Position F.* Stand at the edge of the grass on the shortstop side of the infield (see figure 7.2). This is similar to position C (see figure 6.1c on page 80).

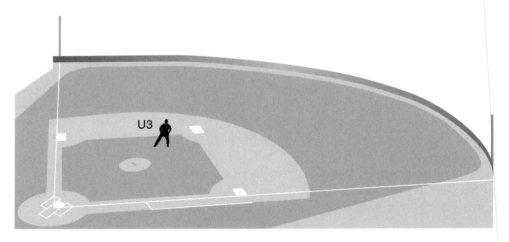

FIGURE 7.2   U3 in position F.

- *Position G.* Stand behind second base at or near the edge of the dirt. You can be on the shortstop side of the infield (see figure 7.3).

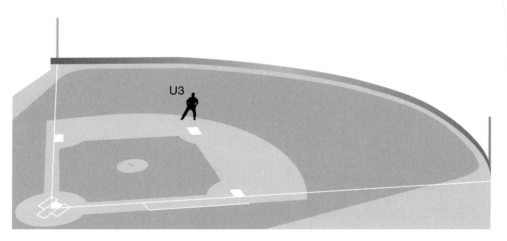

FIGURE 7.3   U3 in position G.

Basic coverage in a four-umpire crew is similar to that used in the three-umpire system with these three major exceptions, all of which refer to U3. When you are the second-base umpire, make sure that you

- cover the steal play at second from the inside position (position F),
- are in position F when there is a possibility of a double play and
- use position F with a runner at second base and no runner at first base.

General Duties and Responsibilities

Here we'll cover the general duties and responsibilities of all four umpires. We'll start with the plate umpire.

U1 Responsibilities

U1's general responsibilities are as follows:

- *Balls and strikes.* You call these.
- *Checked swings.* Appeal checked swings on right-handed batters to U2 and on left-handed batters to U4.
- *Fair or foul calls.* Rule fair or foul on any batted ball down either the first- or third-base line when the ball is played or when it comes to rest in front of the front edge of the base.
- *Catch or no-catch calls.* Rule catch or no catch on all foul fly balls behind home plate and up to the first- and third-base bags, on any fly balls taken by the catcher, and on fly balls or line drives to the pitcher.
- *Batted balls.* When the batter hits the ball, move out from behind the plate to watch plays and to be ready to move to a base to cover a play if either U2 or U4 goes out or moves to cover second base. Watch every play as if it were yours to call, both because your partners might appeal to you for help and because as umpire-in-chief you might be required to decide on play situations involving rules.
- *Infield-fly rule and time plays.* Signal your partners in an infield-fly situation and when a two-out time play is possible.
- *Tag-ups.* Move to cover the tag-up by a runner on third advancing home after a fly ball hit to left field.

U2 Responsibilities

Remember to move one or two steps toward the plate with the pitch so that when the ball is hit, you are ready to move and cover any play for which you are responsible. Here are your basic responsibilities:

- *Calls at first.* Make calls at first base on plays in the infield.
- *Fair or foul calls.* Rule fair or foul on ground balls down the first-base line from the front of the bag to the foul pole, especially on balls bounding over the bag, and on fly balls from the bag to the foul pole.
- *Catch or no-catch calls.* Rule catch or no catch on fly balls and line drives in the infield taken by the first or second baseman when U3 is in position E or G and when the first baseman and the second baseman are moving toward first when U3 is in position F. Also make these calls on fly balls to the outfield in which the right fielder moves toward his foul line.
- *Checked swings.* Respond only if U1 asks for help. U1 should appeal to you on right-handers.
- *Batter-runner.* Be ready to move to cover the batter-runner advancing to second base if U4 has to stay at third base to cover an advancing runner and U3 has gone out on a fly ball.

Uniqueness of a Four-Umpire Crew

You have been selected to umpire at your state tournament—quite an honor. Along with the honor comes a bit of pressure, and not simply because you're umpiring at tournament games. You find that you're to be part of a four-umpire crew, and chances are good that you have not been part of such a crew during the regular season. The pressure comes with the uniqueness of the situation.

Most people might think that it's easier to be part of a four-umpire crew—that is, the more umpires, the merrier. Although a four-umpire crew means that each umpire covers a little less ground, it can also cause coverage and rotation confusion because your duties and responsibilities are slightly different from those you are accustomed to with smaller crews.

The key is to be thoroughly familiar with your responsibilities in a four-umpire crew before you find yourself in such a crew. Study this chapter well and become familiar with the rotations of a four-umpire crew.

U3 Responsibilities

Remember to move one or two steps toward the plate with the pitch so that when the batter hits the ball, you are ready to move and cover any play for which you are responsible.

- *Catch or no-catch calls.* Rule catch or no catch on all fly balls between the left and right fielders if you are in position E or G. Go out on any fly ball other than a simple, routine catch. If you're in position F, don't go out on a fly ball. U2 and U4 will split fly-ball coverage (similar to what occurs in three-man mechanics) when you're in position F.
- *Calls at second base.* Come into the infield on base hits to make calls at second base.
- *Positioning.* With first base occupied and a potential steal play at second, assume position F to get the best angle on the steal play at second. Typically, be on either side of second base at the edge of the grass. Be on the right-field side if the batter is right-handed and vice versa. With a runner at second, be on the right-field side. With second base occupied, assume position G, from which you will cover pickoff attempts or other plays at second and be able to go out to rule catch or no catch on tough calls in the outfield. When you're in position F, rule catch or no catch on fly balls and line drives to the shortstop or second baseman that move them toward second base.

U4 Responsibilities

Remember to move one or two steps with the pitch so that when the ball is hit, you are ready to move to cover any play for which you are responsible. Here are your basic responsibilities:

- *Calls at third base.* Make calls at third base on plays in the infield—runners advancing or returning on batted balls, pickoffs, and tag-ups by runners on fly balls to center or right field.
- *Fair or foul calls.* Rule fair or foul on ground balls down the third-base line from the front of the bag to the foul pole, especially on balls bounding over the bag, and on fly balls from the bag to the left-field foul pole.
- *Catch or no-catch calls.* Rule catch or no catch on fly balls and line drives in the infield fielded by the third baseman or the shortstop if U3 is in position E or G or if the third baseman or shortstop is moving toward third base and U3 is in position F. Also make these calls on fly balls to the outfield in which the left fielder moves toward his foul line.

- *Batter-runner.* Be ready to move to cover the batter-runner advancing to second base on an extra-base hit if U3 has gone out to rule on a fly ball.
- *Checked swings.* Respond only if U1 asks for help. U1 should appeal to you on left-handers.

Field Mechanics and Coverage

In this section we'll cover all the situations you will face in a four-umpire crew. For each situation, we'll provide the mechanics and coverage for U1, U2, U3 and U4. We'll cover these situations:

- No runners on base
- Runner at first
- Runners at first and second
- Runners at first and third
- Multiple situations (runner at third, runner at second, runners at second and third, bases loaded)

No Runners on Base

In this section we'll outline the coverage for U1, U2, U3 and U4 with no runners on base. Figure 7.4 shows the starting positions of all four umpires.

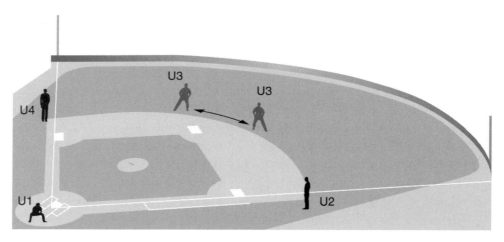

FIGURE 7.4   U1, U2, U3 and U4 starting positions with no runner on base.

U1 Coverage

Besides calling balls and strikes, you have these main duties as plate umpire with no runners on base:

- *All batted balls.* When the ball is hit, move out from behind the plate, both to watch the play and to be ready to move to a base to cover a play at first if U2 goes out or a play at third if U4 goes out.
- *Catch or no-catch calls.* Rule catch or no catch on all foul fly balls behind home plate and up to the first- and third-base bags, on any fly balls that are fielded by the catcher, and on fly balls or line drives to the pitcher.
- *Fair or foul calls.* Rule fair or foul down the first- and third-base lines on any batted ball that is played on or that comes to a rest in front of the front edge of the base.

U2 Coverage

You should be in position A as U2 with the bases empty (page 110). Remember to move one or two steps with the pitch so that when the ball is hit, you are ready to move to make a call for which you are responsible. Here are your main responsibilities:

- *Calls at first base.* Make calls at first base on plays in the infield, including batted balls and putouts.
- *Fair or foul calls.* Rule fair or foul on ground balls down the first-base line from the front of the bag to the right-field foul pole, especially on balls bounding over the bag, and on fly balls from the bag to the foul pole.
- *Catch or no-catch calls.* Rule catch or no catch on fly balls and line drives in the infield fielded by the first or second baseman and on fly balls to the outfield in which the right fielder moves toward his foul line.
- *Batter-runner.* Be ready to move to cover the batter-runner advancing to second base if U4 has to stay to cover third base, and U3 has gone out on a fly ball.
- *Calls at home plate.* Be ready to cover home plate if U1 has moved to cover third on a triple.

U3 Coverage

As U3 you should be in position E (page 110) with no runners on base. Be on the outfield side of second base and on the pull side of the batter. You rule catch or no catch on all fly balls between the left and right fielders. Go out on any outfield catch other than a routine catch (see figure 7.5); the wing umpires will cover for you. Come into the infield on base hits to make calls at second base.

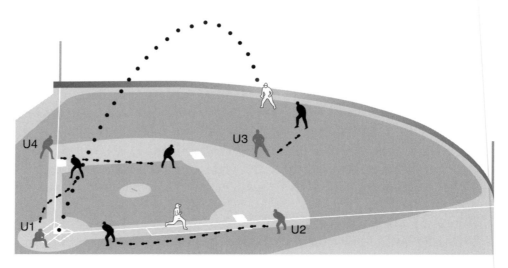

FIGURE 7.5   U3 going out on a fly ball.

U4 Coverage

As the third-base umpire with the bases empty, you should be in position D (see page 110). Be sure to move with the pitch to be ready to move in any direction and to make a call for which you are responsible. Also be ready to make these calls:

- *Fair or foul calls.* Rule fair or foul on ground balls down the third-base line from the front of the bag to the left-field foul pole, especially on balls bounding over the bag, and on fly balls from the bag to the foul pole.
- *Catch or no-catch calls.* Rule catch or no catch on fly balls and line drives in the infield that are fielded by the third baseman or short-stop and on fly balls to the outfield in which the left fielder moves toward his foul line.
- *Batter-runner.* Be ready to move to cover the batter-runner advancing to second base on an extra-base hit if U3 has gone out to rule on a fly ball.

Runner at First Base

With a runner at first base, the four umpires should be in the starting positions shown in figure 7.6.

U1 Coverage

As the home plate umpire you will call balls and strikes and make these calls as well:

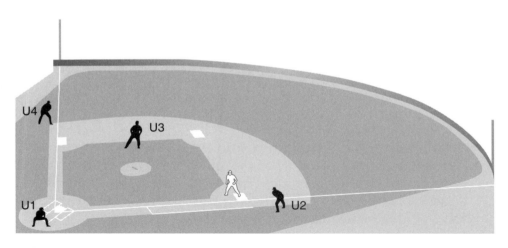

FIGURE 7.6   U1, U2, U3 and U4 starting positions with a runner at first.

- *Fair or foul calls.* Rule fair or foul on any batted ball down the first- or third-base line when the ball is played on or comes to rest in front of the front edge of the base.
- *Catch or no-catch calls.* Rule catch or no catch on all foul fly balls behind home plate and up to the first- and third-base bags, on any fly balls that are fielded by the catcher, and on fly balls or line drives to the pitcher.
- *Vacant bases.* Move to cover the vacant bag if either wing umpire goes out (see figure 7.7). You will be responsible for the touch or tag at first by R1 if U2 goes out.

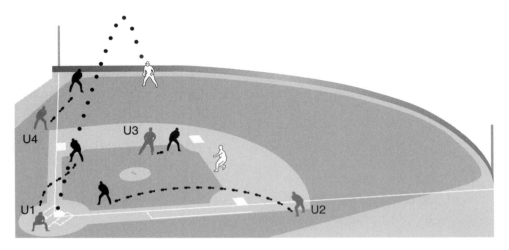

FIGURE 7.7   U1 going to cover third as U4 goes out on a fly ball to left field.

U2 Coverage

You'll be in position A (see figure 7.6) as U2 with a runner on first, but you'll have moved some from your position with no runners on. With a runner on first, you should have both feet in foul territory, 6 to 8 feet behind the first baseman, and be in position to make a call on an attempted pickoff. Your coverage responsibilities are these:

- *Attempted pickoffs.* In the aforementioned position, you can set up to get the angle on an attempted pickoff. You should be able to look through the runner, the bag and the first baseman toward the pitcher. Watch for balks on pickoff attempts. Signal safe or out on a pickoff play only if the fielder makes a tag.
- *Calls at first base.* Move to make all calls at first base on plays in the infield.
- *Batter-runner.* Watch the batter-runner touch first on a base hit; be ready to release the batter-runner and move to cover home if U1 has gone to cover third base. Make the call on the runner returning to first in a rundown from the outside position.
- *Fair or foul calls.* Call fair or foul on ground balls past the front edge of the first-base bag and on balls bounding over the bag. Move to call foul fly balls past first.
- *Catch or no-catch calls.* Rule catch or no catch on fly balls to right in which the right fielder moves to his left and on all fly balls or line drives fielded by the first baseman or the second baseman moving toward first base. Go out on tough calls.
- *Checked swings.* Be alert to help on checked swings by right-handed batters if asked by U1.

U3 Coverage

As U3 you will be in position F (see figure 7.6) with a runner on first. Be opposite the pull side of the batter. You will be near the dirt on the shortstop side of second to cover a steal attempt or force-out. You will make these calls with a runner on first:

- *Calls at second base.* Make all calls on plays at second base. Be alert for illegal slides or interference at second base on double plays. On a rundown play at second base, use inside position.
- *Attempted steals.* Turn with the catcher's throw to make the call on a steal attempt at second base.
- *Catch or no-catch calls.* Call catch or no catch on fly balls between left and right field and on fly balls or line drives fielded by the shortstop or second baseman, unless they are moving toward the foul line on their respective sides. Do not leave the infield.

U4 Coverage

As U4 you should be in position D (see figure 7.6 on page 113) with a runner on first base, ready to make these calls:

- *Calls at third base.* Move to make all calls at third base on plays in the infield. In rundown situations, make the call on the runner advancing or returning to third base.
- *Catch or no-catch calls.* Call catch or no catch on fly balls to left field in which the left fielder moves to his right, on fly balls and line drives fielded by the third baseman or the shortstop moving toward the third base line, and on foul fly balls past the third-base bag. Go out on tough calls.
- *Fair or foul calls.* Call fair or foul on ground balls from the front edge of the third-base bag and on balls bounding over the bag. Move to make the call on any fly balls past the third-base bag.
- *Checked swings.* Be alert to help on checked swings by left-handed batters if asked by U1.

Runners at First and Second

Umpire starting positions with runners at first and second are shown in figure 7.8.

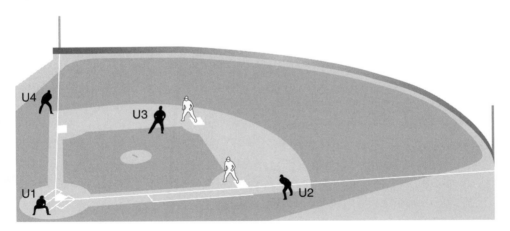

FIGURE 7.8 U1, U2, U3 and U4 starting positions with runners at first and second.

U1 Coverage

Besides your ball and strike calls, you will have these duties as home plate umpire with runners at first and second:

- *Fair or foul calls.* Rule fair or foul down the first- and third-base lines on any batted balls that are played on or that come to a stop in front of the front edge of the bag.

- *Catch or no-catch calls.* Rule catch or no catch on all foul fly balls behind home plate and up to the first- and third-base bags, on any fly balls fielded by the catcher, and on fly balls or line drives to the pitcher.
- *Vacant bases.* Move to cover a vacant bag if either wing umpire goes out or leaves to cover another base.

U2 Coverage

As first-base umpire with runners at first and second, you will be in position A (page 115) with both feet in foul territory, 6 to 8 feet behind the first baseman. Your coverage duties include the following:

- *Pickoff attempts.* In the position just described you will have a good angle on pickoff attempts—one in which you can look through the runner, the bag and the first baseman to the pitcher. Watch for balks on pickoff attempts. Signal safe or out on a pickoff play only if the fielder makes a tag.
- *Calls at first base.* Move to make all calls at first base on plays in the infield. Make the call from the outside position on the runner returning to first in a rundown.
- *Batter-runner.* Watch the batter-runner touch first on a base hit; be ready to release batter-runner and move to cover home if U1 has gone to cover third base.
- *Fair or foul calls.* Call fair or foul on ground balls past the front edge of the first-base bag and on balls bounding over the bag. Move to call foul fly balls past first.
- *Catch or no-catch calls.* Rule catch or no catch on fly balls to right in which the right fielder moves to his left and on all fly balls or line drives fielded by the first baseman or the second baseman moving toward first base. Go out on tough calls.

U3 Coverage

You'll be in position F (page 115) when you're second-base umpire with runners on first and second. You should be on the right side of second. Your main responsibilities are the following:

- *Pickoff attempts.* Watch for pickoff attempts at second base.
- *Calls at second base.* Make all calls at second base except tag-ups of the advancing R2 if you have gone out on a fly ball. Be alert for illegal slides or interference at second base on double plays.
- *Catch or no-catch calls.* Call catch or no catch on fly balls between left and right field or on fly balls or line drives fielded by the shortstop or the second baseman unless they are moving toward the foul line on their respective sides. Go out on tough calls.

- *Base runners.* If U4 goes out to rule on a fly ball, move to cover R1 returning to second base. U1 will be at third for the possible advance. If U2 goes out to rule on a fly ball, move to cover R2 advancing to second.

U4 Coverage
As third-base umpire with runners at first and second, you should be in position D (see page 115). Your primary responsibilities are these:

- *Calls at third base.* Move to make all calls at third base on plays in the infield. In rundown situations, make the call on a runner advancing or returning to third base.
- *Catch or no-catch calls.* Call catch or no catch on fly balls to left field in which the left fielder moves to his right, on fly balls and line drives fielded by the third baseman or the shortstop moving toward the third-base line, and on foul fly balls past the third-base bag. Go out on tough calls.
- *Fair or foul calls.* Call fair or foul on ground balls from the front edge of the third-base bag and on balls bounding over the bag. Move to make the call on fly balls past the third-base bag.
- *Calls at second base.* Be alert to move to cover second base if U3 has gone out to rule on a play.

Runners at First and Third
With runners at first and third, the umpires should be in the starting positions shown in figure 7.9.

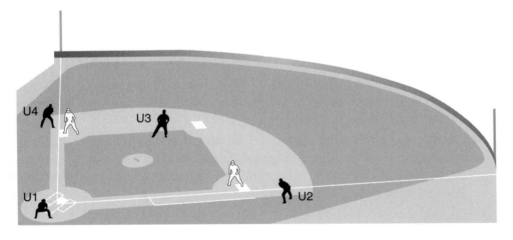

FIGURE 7.9   U1, U2, U3 and U4 starting positions with runners at first and third.

U1 Coverage

Besides calling balls and strikes, you should be prepared to make these calls as home plate umpire with runners at first and third:

- *Plays at the plate.* Your movement will be limited with runners at first and third because of the high potential for a play at the plate. On a base hit down the line, you may move to cover at third.
- *Fair or foul calls.* Rule fair or foul on any batted ball down the first- or third-base line that is played on or that comes to rest in front of the front edge of the base.
- *Catch or no-catch calls.* Rule catch or no catch on all foul fly balls behind home plate and up to the first- and third-base bags, on any fly balls fielded by the catcher, and on fly balls or line drives to the pitcher.
- *Tag-ups.* Move to line up the tag-up by R1 at third on a fly ball to left field and when U4 has the catch or no-catch call.

U2 Coverage

As the first-base umpire you will be in position A (page 117), about 6 to 8 feet behind the first baseman. As always, be alert on checked swings by right-handed batters so that you can help if U1 asks. You have these basic calls with runners on first and third:

- *Pickoff plays.* Get a good angle on the pickoff. Signal safe or out on a pickoff attempt only if the fielder makes a tag.
- *Calls at first base.* Move to make all calls at first base on plays in the infield. Make the call from the outside position on a runner returning to first in a rundown.
- *Batter-runner.* Watch the batter-runner touch first on a base hit; be ready to release the batter-runner and move to cover home if U1 has gone to cover third base (see figure 7.10).
- *Fair or foul calls.* Call fair or foul on ground balls past the front edge of the first-base bag and on balls bounding over the bag. Move to call foul fly balls past first.
- *Catch or no-catch calls.* Rule catch or no catch on fly balls to right in which the right fielder moves to his left and on all fly balls or line drives fielded by the first baseman or the second baseman moving toward first base. Go out on tough calls.

U3 Coverage

As the second-base umpire you will be opposite the pull side of the batter in position F (page 117) with runners on first and third, near the dirt on

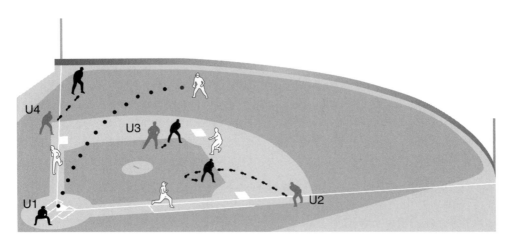

FIGURE 7.10   U2 watching first and preparing for a possible play at home.

the shortstop side of second to cover steal attempts and force-outs. You are responsible for these calls:

- *Calls at second base.* Make all calls on plays at second base. Be alert for illegal slides or interference at second base on double plays. On rundown plays at second base, use the inside position.
- *Steal attempts.* Turn with the catcher's throw to make the call on a steal attempt at second base.
- *Catch or no-catch calls.* Call catch or no catch on fly balls between left and right field and on fly balls or line drives fielded by the shortstop or second baseman unless they are moving toward the foul line on their respective sides (see figure 7.11). Do not leave the infield.

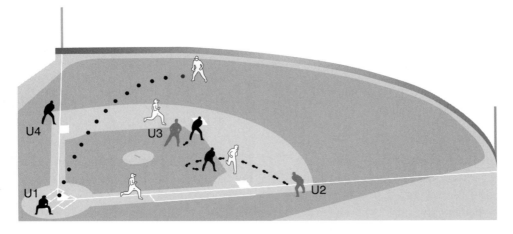

FIGURE 7.11   U3 making a catch or no-catch call on a fly ball.

- *Base runners.* If U2 or U4 goes out to rule on a fly ball, move to cover R2 or R1 returning to base after the catch.

U4 Coverage

When you are the third-base umpire with runners on first and third, you will be in position D with both feet in foul territory, 6 to 8 feet behind the third baseman (see page 117). As always, be alert on checked swings by left-handed batters so that you can help if U1 asks. You have these other responsibilities:

- *Calls at third base.* Move to make all calls at third base on plays in the infield. In rundown situations, make the call on a runner advancing or returning to third base.
- *Pickoff attempts.* Set up to get a good angle on a pickoff attempt at third. Signal safe or out only if the fielder makes a tag.
- *Tag-ups.* Move to line up the tag-up by R1 at third advancing on a fly ball to center or right field or on a fly ball in which the left fielder moves toward center.
- *Catch or no-catch calls.* Call catch or no catch on fly balls to left field in which the left fielder moves to his right, on fly balls and line drives fielded by the third baseman or the shortstop moving toward the third-base line, and on foul fly balls past the third-base bag. Go out on tough calls.
- *Fair or foul calls.* Call fair or foul on ground balls from the front edge of the third-base bag and on balls bounding over the bag. Move to make the call on fly balls past the third-base bag.

Multiple Situations

This section covers your responsibilities in multiple situations:

- Runner at third only
- Runner at second only
- Runners at second and third
- Bases loaded

For umpire starting positions with a runner at third and with runners on second and third, see figure 7.12. For umpire starting positions with a runner on second, see figure 7.13. For umpire starting positions with the bases loaded, see figure 7.14.

Following are coverage responsibilities for all four umpires in the aforementioned situations.

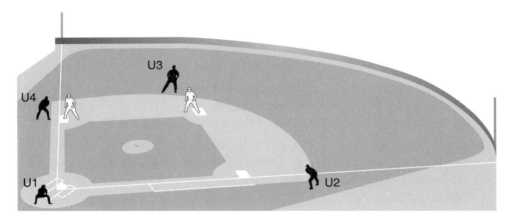

FIGURE 7.12   U1, U2, U3 and U4 starting positions with runners on second and third.

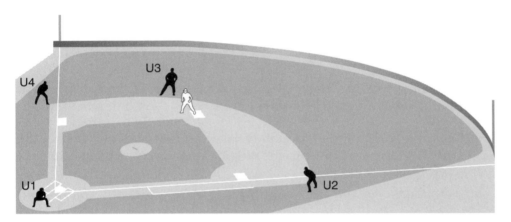

FIGURE 7.13   U1, U2, U3 and U4 starting positions with a runner on second.

FIGURE 7.14   U1, U2, U3 and U4 starting positions with the bases loaded.

U1 Coverage

Besides calling balls and strikes, you will also be responsible for these calls:

- *Fair or foul calls.* Rule fair or foul down the first- and third-base lines up to the front edge of the bags on any batted ball that is played on or that comes to rest in front of the front edge of the bag.
- *Catch or no-catch calls.* Rule catch or no catch on all foul fly balls behind home plate and up to the first- and third-base bags, on any fly balls that are fielded by the catcher, and on fly balls or line drives to the pitcher.
- *Tag-ups.* Move to line up the tag-up of R1 at third base on a fly ball to left field or if U4 has the catch or no-catch call.
- *Plays at the plate.* Your movement will be limited because of the potential play at the plate and will remain limited until the lead runner has scored. If U4 goes out, move to cover not only a tag-up at third but also any succeeding plays at third.

U2 Coverage

Your coverage with a runner at third, a runner at second, runners at second and third, and the bases loaded includes these responsibilities:

- *Calls at first base.* Move to make all calls at first base on plays in the infield. Make the call from the outside position on a runner returning to first in a rundown.
- *Pickoff attempts.* Set up to get the angle on a pickoff attempt and watch for a balk on the attempt. Signal safe or out on a pickoff only if the fielder makes a tag.
- *Batter-runner.* Watch the batter-runner touch first on a base hit; be ready to release the batter-runner and move to cover home if U1 has gone to cover third base.
- *Fair or foul calls.* Call fair or foul on ground balls past the front edge of the first-base bag and on balls bounding over the bag. Move to call foul fly balls past first.
- *Catch or no-catch calls.* Rule catch or no catch on fly balls to right in which the right fielder moves to his left and on all fly balls or line drives fielded by the first baseman or the second baseman moving toward first base. Go out on tough calls.

U3 Coverage

Your position depends on the base-runner situation; see figures 7.12-7.14 for positioning. Your responsibilities with a runner at third, a runner at second, runners at second and third, and the bases loaded are the following:

- *Pickoff attempts.* Watch for pickoff attempts at second base.
- *Calls at second base.* Make all calls at second base except tag-ups of the advancing R2 if you have gone out on a fly ball. Be alert for illegal slides or interference at second base on double plays.
- *Catch or no-catch calls.* Call catch or no catch on fly balls between left and right field or on fly balls or line drives fielded by the shortstop or second baseman unless they are moving toward the foul line on their respective sides. Go out on tough calls.
- *Base runners.* If U4 goes out to rule on a fly ball, move to cover R2 or R1 returning to a base after a catch. If U2 goes out to rule on a fly ball, move to cover R2 or R3 returning to a base after a catch.

U4 Coverage

You should be in position D, about 10 feet behind the third baseman and in foul territory, when you are umpiring at third base with a runner on second base. When a lone runner is on third, when runners are on second and third, and when the bases are loaded, you should be closer to the third baseman, about 6 to 8 feet behind him, in line with the pitcher. (See figures 7.12-7.14 on page 121.)

Your main responsibilities are these:

- *Calls at third base.* Move to make all calls at third base on plays in the infield. In rundown situations, make the call on a runner advancing or returning to third base.
- *Catch or no-catch calls.* Call catch or no catch on fly balls to left field in which the left fielder moves to his right, on fly balls and line drives fielded by the third baseman or the shortstop moving toward the third-base line, and on foul fly balls past the third-base bag. Go out on tough calls.
- *Fair or foul calls.* Call fair or foul on ground balls from the front edge of the third-base bag and on balls bounding over the bag. Move to make the call on fly balls past the third-base bag.
- *Calls at second base.* Be alert to move to cover second base if U3 has gone out to rule catch or no catch.

Now that you've completed the section on mechanics, it's time to test yourself on your knowledge of the rules and consider how you'd rule in various situations. That's exactly what you'll do in the next four chapters.

PART III

APPLYING THE RULES

CHAPTER 8

PROCEDURES, TERMS AND CONDUCT

As you know from your *NFHS Baseball Rules Book,* there are 10 main rules that cover all areas of play. These are:

- Rule 1: Players, Field and Equipment
- Rule 2: Playing Terms and Definitions
- Rule 3: Substituting, Coaching, Bench and Field Conduct
- Rule 4: Starting and Ending the Game
- Rule 5: Dead Ball and Suspension of Play
- Rule 6: Pitching
- Rule 7: Batting
- Rule 8: Baserunning
- Rule 9: Scoring and Record Keeping
- Rule 10: Umpiring

In the next four chapters we'll consider various cases regarding those 10 rules. For each rule we'll present several cases and provide, at the end of the chapter, the appropriate rulings to the cases. The references to the rules, of course, are meant to supplement your close study of the *NFHS Baseball Rules Book* and bring to life some of the situations you will face as an umpire. By no means, however, are they meant to replace your need to know the *NFHS Baseball Rules Book* thoroughly. Make sure that you are well-versed in all the rules as spelled out in the *NFHS Baseball Rules Book* and use chapters 8 through 11 to test and augment your understanding of the rules.

In this chapter we'll consider cases in the first three rules.

Rule 1: Players, Field and Equipment

Rule 1 covers a wide expanse of ground in terms of players, field and equipment rules. Here we'll present several scenarios and rulings related to those issues. Consider how you would respond in each situation and check your judgments against the answers beginning on page 132.

CASE 1: Unlisted Substitute

You're the plate umpire for a game between Pittsfield and Jamestown. During the pregame conference, the coach of each team hands you a lineup card. Pittsfield, the visiting team, has all its eligible players listed—the starters and all possible substitutes. Jamestown's coach, on the other hand, has listed only his starting lineup.

Pittsfield plates five runs in the top of the first, all off Jamestown's starting pitcher. In the bottom of the first Jamestown gets a rally of its own going, scoring two runs and loading the bases with two outs. The Jamestown coach decides to pinch hit for his pitcher and sends up a player to do so. Of course, this player is not listed on their lineup card; the Jamestown coach had listed only his starting nine.

The Pittsfield manager comes out to protest, saying that the player is ineligible to pinch hit because he wasn't listed on the card. What's your call?

CASE 2: Removing a Batting Helmet

You're the field umpire in a game between Brownsburg and York. In the bottom of the sixth the York first baseman clubs a double to deep center field, driving in three runs and giving his team a one-run lead in a key conference game. In jubilation, the York player, standing on second base after the play is over, takes off his helmet and tosses it in the air, whooping as he catches it and raising an arm toward his teammates in the dugout.

Do you have a call to make here? If so, what is it?

Also consider two other situations involving helmets. What if the York player had lifted his helmet to adjust its fit, not lifting it above his temples before replacing it? What if the York batboy, not wearing a helmet, left the dugout to retrieve a ball between home plate and the backstop?

CASE 3: Catcher's Helmet

You're the plate umpire in a game at Centralia. The Westwood catcher takes his place in the bottom of the first with a mask and a catcher's helmet that do not have a NOCSAE stamp. The Centralia coach notices this and complains to you that the mask and helmet must meet NOCSAE standards to be used. How do you respond?

CASE 4: Double First Base

You're umpiring at first base in a game between Richmond and Independence. (The state association has adopted use of a double first base.) In the top of the fifth with a runner on first, a Richmond batter drives a ball to left-center field. The runner on first rounds second and goes to third while the batter touches the white part of first base, heads toward second, sees that he won't make it and returns to first, his foot touching only the colored part of the base just before the first baseman receives the relay throw and applies the tag. The batter-runner's foot remains on the colored part of first base. Is the batter-runner safe or out?

It is your duty as an umpire to verify that a catcher's helmet is marked with a NOCSAE stamp and meets NOCSAE standards.

Now consider these similar situations: The Richmond batter touches only the colored part of first base and cruises in safely to second with a double. The Independence shortstop relays the throw to the first baseman, who steps on the white part of the bag. Is the batter-runner safe or out?

What if the batter-runner had touched the white part of the first-base bag and made it safely to second? Would this situation result in a different call?

Rule 2: Playing Terms and Definitions

Rule 2 covers a variety of situations that can and do happen on the field. Following are several examples of those situations. As you read them, consider how you would call them and then refer to the answers beginning on page 133.

CASE 5: Ball Hits Umpire

You're umpiring at second base in a four-umpire crew. With the bases empty a Westwood hitter hits a line drive up the middle. The line drive is touched in flight by the Pittsfield second baseman before it hits you and rebounds to the shortstop, who catches the ball before it hits the ground. The batter-runner then crosses first base while the shortstop holds the ball in the air, waiting for your out call. Is the batter-runner safe or out?

CASE 6: Securing the Ball for an Out

You're umpiring at first base in the bottom of the seventh inning in a tie game between York and Richmond. The first Richmond batter steps up to the plate and hits a ground ball straight to shortstop. The shortstop scoops up the ball and fires it to first, beating the batter-runner by nearly two steps, but the first baseman juggles the ball and it rolls up in his arm. In desperation, he clamps the ball close to his body with his elbow; it's securely clamped to his body before the batter-runner touches the bag. The first baseman then extracts the ball from the crook of his elbow and shows you the ball, indicating he had it held securely against his body.

You call the batter-runner safe, causing the York coach to run out to protest. Was your call correct, or does the York coach have grounds to protest?

CASE 7: Touching a Foul Ball While in Fair Territory

You're umpiring at third base in a game between Westwood and Brownsburg. A Westwood hitter lifts a looping fly ball down the left-field line and the Brownsburg left fielder races over and reaches for the ball as it's about to drop onto the field. As he makes a reach for the ball, his body is in fair territory, but the ball and his glove are in foul territory. The ball glances off his glove and lands in foul territory. Is the ball fair or foul?

CASE 8: Ball Kicked by Batter-Runner

Centralia is playing Independence, and you're umpiring at first base. With two outs in the bottom of the second inning, the Centralia batter strikes out, but the ball glances off the Independence catcher's glove and bounces a short way down the first-base line. The Centralia batter takes off for first and accidentally kicks the ball as he runs. He makes it safely to first as the catcher scampers after the ball and, after tracking it down, fires too late to first base. You call the batter-runner safe. The Independence coach hustles out to protest the call, saying that the batter should be out because he kicked the ball. Otherwise, he says, his catcher could have fielded it easily and thrown the batter out. How do you respond?

Rule 3: Substituting, Coaching, Bench and Field Conduct

Rule 3 covers rules involved in making proper substitutions, bench and field conduct, and various situations and plays that you will face on the field. Consider the calls you would make in the following situations and then check your judgments against the answers beginning on page 134.

CASE 9: Substitute Re-Entering the Game

You're behind the plate for a game between Richmond and Jamestown. Smith is a Jamestown player who entered the game in the top of the third inning as a relief pitcher. He pitches a third of an inning, getting the final out, and then does not play or take the field after that relief appearance in the third.

Now, in the bottom of the sixth, Smith again appears, this time as a pinch hitter for Jamestown. The pitcher makes one pitch to Smith before the Richmond coach, realizing what is happening, comes to the plate to say that Smith is an illegal batter. What's your call?

What if the Jamestown coach was the one who realized what was happening and called Smith back to the dugout after that first pitch? What if neither coach realized that Smith had already entered and exited as a substitute, but you knew it?

CASE 10: Discovering an Illegal Substitute After the Fact

With two outs in the top of the sixth inning in a game in which you're the home plate umpire, a Pittsfield batter hits a double off the York pitcher. The next batter hits a home run over the left-field fence. As the batter crosses the plate, the York coach realizes that the Pittsfield runner on second, who had doubled only moments earlier, was an illegal substitute. (He had already entered and exited the game as a substitute.) The York coach comes out to protest, informing you that the runner on second was an illegal substitute. What is your decision?

CASE 11: Third-Base Coach Hit by Thrown Ball

With a runner on first, a Brownsburg batter laces a single to right field. The Brownsburg runner on first rounds second and heads to third, where you have the call. The ball is thrown off line and hits the third-base coach before he can get out of the way. The coach is in the coach's box. What is your call?

Now consider these situations: What would your call be if the coach was standing in foul territory but not in the coach's box? What would your call be if he was standing in fair territory?

CASE 12: Hurdling the Catcher

You're behind the plate as a Westwood runner is attempting to score against Independence. The runner approaches home as the catcher, on his knees, is about to receive the ball. The runner hurdles the catcher and touches home plate before the catcher can make the tag. Is this a legal play?

Answers

Here we've provided the correct answers to each situation. Check your responses to see how you did.

Case 1: Unlisted Substitute

The Pittsfield manager protested the use of a Jamestown player who was not listed on the lineup card. Use of that player, however, is legal. Not listing substitutes' names on a lineup card is not a violation.

Case 2: Removing a Batting Helmet

The York batter who just doubled and then removed his helmet in celebration is in violation of the rules and should be penalized. (For the first offense by a team, the batter would be warned. If his team had been warned previously, the batter would be ejected and a teammate would replace him as a base runner at second base.) If the York batter had lifted his helmet, but not past his temples, there would be no violation. The batboy who came onto the field without a helmet should be warned, and any subsequent violation could result in his not being allowed on the field. This rule would apply to anyone shagging balls in a live-ball area, even if the ball was dead. This rule is in place for safety.

If an illegal substitute is discovered after the fact, it is still appropriate to call the player out.

Case 3: Catcher's Helmet

The Westwood catcher who had a mask and helmet without a NOCSAE stamp is in violation of the rules. As of January 1, 2003, all catcher's masks and helmets must meet the NOCSAE standard (this standard requires dual earflaps on the helmet). Again, this rule is in place to promote players' safety.

Coaches are required to secure a legal mask and helmet combination. If they do not have proper equipment, they should ask the opponent if they can borrow some legal equipment for the catcher. If that isn't possible, the game cannot continue. Notify your state association, and they will determine what will happen next. A game can't continue if illegal equipment is discovered to be in use.

Case 4: Double First Base

The Richmond batter-runner who was tagged by the first baseman while the batter-runner's foot was on the colored part of the bag is out. The colored base is used only on the initial contact with the base for the players' safety. Once that portion of the play is over, the batter-runner must use the white portion of the bag. If the Richmond batter touches only the colored part of the first-base bag and cruises safely into second with a double, he is safe. Likewise, he is safe if he touches only the white part of first base and makes it safely to second. He can touch the white side of the base as long as he doesn't interfere with the fielder at first base.

Case 5: Ball Hits Umpire

The Westwood batter who hit the line drive that deflected off you to the shortstop is safe, even though the shortstop caught the ball before it hit the ground. Any batted ball that stays in play cannot be caught for an out if it hits an umpire. The ball remains alive because the second baseman touched it before it hit you; the shortstop could have attempted to throw the batter-runner out at first base as in a conventional ground-ball situation.

If the ball had hit you before it touched a defensive player, you would declare the ball dead and award the batter first base.

Case 6: Securing the Ball for an Out

In calling the Richmond runner safe at first even though the York first baseman secured the ball between his elbow and his body, you are correct. A catch is not a catch until the fielder secures the ball with the bare hand or the glove hand.

Case 7: Touching a Foul Ball While in Fair Territory

The ball hit by the Westwood hitter is foul, even though the Brownsburg left fielder touched the ball while he was in fair territory. The judgment depends on the position of the ball, not the position of the fielder. The ball itself was in foul territory. Conversely, if a fielder tries to catch a fly ball near a foul line while he is in foul territory and reaches over in fair territory to catch it, only to have the ball glance off his glove, the ball would be live. Even if the ball lands in foul territory, it is live if a fielder first touched it in fair territory.

Case 8: Ball Kicked by Batter-Runner

You are correct in calling the Centralia batter-runner safe at first because you judged that he accidentally kicked the ball. Had the batter-runner intentionally kicked the ball, he would be called out for interference. But when an offensive player unintentionally kicks a ball, the ball remains live and interference has not occurred.

Case 9: Substitute Re-Entering the Game

No matter who discovers that the Jamestown substitute had re-entered the game after already substituting once and exiting, the player is an illegal substitute and should be called out and restricted to the bench. (Credit the out to the catcher.) The penalty for an ineligible substitute supersedes the penalty for batting out of order.

Case 10: Discovering an Illegal Substitute After the Fact

The York coach has a legitimate gripe, and if you call the runner on second out for being an illegal substitute and restrict that player to the bench or dugout for the duration of the game, you have made the correct call. The home run is nullified and no runs would score because the out on the runner at second base is the third out. The player who hit the home run would lead off the next inning.

Case 11: Third-Base Coach Hit by Thrown Ball

If a thrown ball hits the Brownsburg third-base coach while he is standing in the coach's box, there is no penalty and the ball remains live. The same is true if the coach is in foul territory even if he is out of the coach's box. If, however, he is in fair territory when a thrown ball strikes him, you should call interference, in which case the runner at third is out and the batter-runner remains at first base.

Case 12: Hurdling the Catcher

This play is not legal; the runner is out. If a fielder is not lying on the ground, a runner cannot go over the top of that fielder by hurdling, jumping over him or diving. Such actions are dangerous and, therefore, illegal. A runner may jump or hurdle a fielder who is lying on the ground or hurdle over an outstretched arm, but he can never dive over a fielder. A runner is entitled to slide legally or legally attempt to get around a fielder who has the ball waiting to make the tag.

CHAPTER 9

TIMING

Two main rules cover how to handle time issues *of* a game (Rule 4: Starting and Ending the Game) and *in* a game (Rule 5: Dead Ball and Suspension of Play). We'll explore cases in each of these two rules in this chapter. As in chapter 8 we'll provide the appropriate rulings at the end of the chapter.

Again, remember that these cases should supplement your understanding of the rules, not replace your need to thoroughly know the *NFHS Baseball Rules Book*. Your comprehension of the *NFHS Baseball Rules Book*, with your supplemental studies and on-field experience, will prepare you to make the right calls consistently.

Rule 4: Starting and Ending the Game

Rule 4 delineates procedures for a variety of situations, including pre-game discussions about ground rules, applying the mercy rule, calling games because of darkness or rain, and lineup situations. Following are a few cases taken from Rule 4; decide how you would make the call and then check your decision against the answers beginning on page 138.

CASE 1: Mercy Rule
You're the umpire-in-chief of a game in which the home team, York, is pounding Westwood 19-1 after three innings. Before the fourth inning begins, the Westwood coach, the York coach and you discuss the situation. The state association has adopted the 10-run rule (the mercy rule), but it isn't in effect yet because the game is only beginning the fourth inning.

The Westwood coach and the York coach are both in favor of stopping the contest anyway. What do you do?

CASE 2: Calling a Game for Rain
You're the plate umpire in a game between Richmond and Brownsburg. Rain has been falling lightly on and off throughout the game. At the end of the fifth inning, the score is tied, 6-6. In the top of the sixth Richmond scores a run to go ahead 7-6, but the rain becomes heavy and you halt play. What is the ruling concerning the outcome of the game?

CASE 3: No Substitutes Available

The Pittsfield center fielder injures his ankle in the sixth inning of a game against Independence and has to leave the game. Pittsfield has no eligible substitutes remaining on its bench. What is the ruling in this situation?

Would the situation be different if the Pittsfield player had been ejected from the game for unsporting conduct?

CASE 4: Starters Not at the Field

The Centralia and Jamestown coaches submit their lineups to you, the umpire-in-chief, before the game in Jamestown. But two Centralia starters are not at the field yet; they are on their way, and the Centralia coach is sure that they'll be there in time for the game. He lists them in the eighth and ninth slots on his lineup card to give them a little extra time, just in case. The Jamestown coach says that this arrangement isn't appropriate because the players aren't there yet. How do you rule?

Rule 5: Dead Ball and Suspension of Play

Rule 5 defines when a ball is live and when it's dead, and differentiates between a dead ball and a *delayed* dead ball. Here are a handful of situations involving potential dead-ball plays. Consider how you would respond in each situation and check your judgments against the answers beginning on page 139.

CASE 5: Ball Hitting Runner

York trails 4-3 in the top of the fifth inning in a game against Richmond and has the tying run at second base with no one out. The batter, the York second baseman, is a light hitter, and Richmond is playing in for a sacrifice bunt, expecting York to try to move the runner over to third. Both the Richmond third baseman and the shortstop are playing in front of the runner at second.

The York batter surprises Richmond by swinging away. He hits a ball between the third baseman and the shortstop. As the York runner on second breaks for third, the ball deflects off his foot and bounces into foul territory. The York runner tried to avoid the ball but could not.

Neither the Richmond shortstop nor the third baseman had a chance to play the ball—it was already past them. What is the ruling on the ball that hit the York runner?

CASE 6: Ball Hitting Umpire

Westwood has runners on first and third with no one out in a game against Brownsburg. You are in position behind the pitcher and in front of the

Rule 5 will help you, as an umpire, determine whether a ball is live or dead.

Brownsburg second baseman. The Westwood batter hits a line drive that strikes you (without touching the pitcher first) before you can get out of its way. What is the ruling?

Would the ruling be any different if the line drive had struck you while you were in fair territory behind the third baseman?

CASE 7: Catching a Ball in or Near Dead-Ball Area

In a game against Pittsfield, with runners on second and third and one out, the Richmond left fielder races over beyond the left-field foul line and near the dead-ball area in an attempt to make a catch. He manages to catch the ball with both feet in the playing area, but his momentum carries him so far that he steps with both feet into the dead-ball area. What is your call?

What is the ruling if the left fielder made the catch with one foot on the line marking the dead-ball area and the other foot in the dead-ball area? What is the call if he made the catch with both feet already in the dead-ball area?

CASE 8: Infielder Intentionally Dropping Fly Ball

York is playing Jamestown and has a 6-4 lead in the top of the sixth with a runner on first base and one out. The York batter hits a line drive to the Jamestown second baseman, who intentionally drops the ball and starts a 4-6-3 double play. Is this play a legal double play?

Answers

Following are the answers to the eight cases presented in this chapter.

Case 1: Mercy Rule

The state association has adopted the mercy rule, but it doesn't go into effect until at least four and a half innings have been played. But if both opposing coaches and the umpire-in-chief agree to end the game, it may end. Certainly, in this case, because both coaches want to stop the lopsided game, you have no reason to continue it.

Case 2: Calling a Game for Rain

If the state association has adopted a game-ending procedure in which the game is suspended, it will be continued from the point of suspension with the lineup and batting order for each team the same as the lineup and batting order at the moment of suspension, subject to the rules of the game. If the state association hasn't adopted game-ending procedures for suspended games, a game can be shortened or terminated upon mutual agreement among the opposing coaches and the umpire-in-chief.

It is illegal for a player to intentionally drop a ball, and you should immediately rule the ball dead if this occurs.

Case 3: No Substitutes Available

The Pittsfield center fielder with the injured ankle leaves his team with a deficit. When it is his turn to bat, an automatic out is called and he cannot be replaced if the team has no remaining eligible substitutes. The same conditions would apply if he were ejected for unsporting conduct or if he had to leave the game for any other reason. Pittsfield can continue to play with eight players, but it must finish with eight. If another player had to leave the game, they would have to forfeit the game to Independence.

Case 4: Starters Not at the Field

The Jamestown coach is correct; this arrangement is not allowable. When the coaches exchange lineups, all starters must be at the field. Therefore, you should inform the Centralia coach that he must replace the two starters who are not yet there. If the coach does not have enough players to start the game, the game can be forfeited. (The rules of some state associations state that the previous situation is a no-game and will be played later.)

Case 5: Ball Hitting Runner

Because you judged that the York runner accidentally touched the ball, no violation of the rules occurred and the ball is still live. This is the case when a batted ball has passed a fielder other than the pitcher; no other fielder has a play on the ball and the touching of the ball is accidental. If you had judged that the runner intentionally deflected the batted ball, you would call interference and declare the ball dead and the runner out. In that case, the batter would be credited with a base hit and placed on first.

Case 6: Ball Hitting Umpire

When the line drive struck you while you were behind the pitcher and in front of the second baseman, you would be correct if you ruled the ball to be dead. The runner on third would remain there. The runner on first would go to second because he was forced to advance by the batter-runner, who would be entitled to first base. If, however, you had been in position behind the third baseman and the line drive struck you, the ball would be live because it passed a fielder (the third baseman).

Case 7: Catching a Ball in or Near Dead-Ball Area

The Richmond left fielder caught the ball with both feet in the playing area and then his momentum took him fully into dead-ball area. The catch is allowed, and the ball becomes dead when the player moves into dead-ball area. The Pittsfield runners on second and third are each allowed to move up a base (thus a run scores). If the left fielder made the catch with one foot on the line marking the dead-ball area and the other foot in the dead-ball area, it is a legal catch and the runners can move up at their risk. If the left fielder made the catch with both feet already in the dead-ball area, it is not a catch. It's a dead ball, and the runners return to their bases.

Case 8: Infielder Intentionally Dropping Fly Ball

The Jamestown second baseman cannot intentionally drop a line drive (or any ball in the air). This play gives the defense an unfair advantage over the offense, because the base runner is not going to run on a ball that he believes will be caught in the air in the infield. Rule the ball dead as soon as the second baseman intentionally drops it and call the batter out. The runner returns to first base.

CHAPTER 10

PLAY

We've looked at cases, in previous chapters, that have to do with the first five rules of your *NFHS Baseball Rules Book*. In this chapter we'll consider some cases that have to do with the next three rules—those covering pitching, batting and baserunning. As with the cases in the previous chapters, the answers appear at the end of the chapter.

Rule 6: Pitching

Rule 6 concerns legal and illegal pitches, the timing of pitches, time allotted to warm up and other matters related to pitching, but above all it concerns the many rules pertaining to committing a balk. Pitchers can commit a balk in many ways, and in numerous situations, people think a balk has been committed when it has not. The balk call is one of the least-understood calls in baseball, at least by fans and by some coaches and players. Therefore, thoroughly familiarize yourself with the rules on balks as well as other aspects of pitching.

Here we'll present some cases that address some of those elements of pitching. Decide how you would rule and then check your decisions against the answers beginning on page 145.

CASE 1: Pitching After Balking
Richmond has a runner on third against Jamestown with two outs in the top of the fourth. The count is three balls and two strikes on the Richmond batter. The Jamestown pitcher balks but still delivers the pitch—which sails over the catcher's head. The batter, however, swings and misses as the ball sails back to the backstop, and the runner on third scampers safely home. The batter beats the throw at first base as well.

What is the call? Would your judgment be any different if the batter did not swing?

CASE 2: Warm-Up Throws
The Westwood pitcher was involved in a rally in the bottom of the second in a game against Brownsburg and is late in getting out to the mound to take his warm-up throws to begin the third. How many warm-up pitches do you allow him to make?

A pitcher is allowed differing numbers of warm-up throws depending on when the pitcher arrives at the mound.

Now consider this situation: The Westwood pitcher was pinch hit for in the second inning, and a relief pitcher replaced him to begin the third. How many warm-up pitches does the relief pitcher get?

CASE 3: Feinting Toward Third Base

Pittsfield has runners on first and third against York with one out in the top of the fifth. The York pitcher comes set, feints toward third with a movement of his shoulder but doesn't step toward third. Do you have a call to make?

Suppose the pitcher makes an arm motion toward third but doesn't step toward third. Instead, he follows with a throw to first base. Do you have a call to make in this situation?

CASE 4: Time Not Granted to Batter

Centralia has a runner on third base. As the Independence pitcher goes into his pitching motion, the Centralia batter requests time, but you, as home-plate umpire, don't grant it. The batter steps out of the box with both feet while the pitcher delivers a pitch—one that would have been clearly out of the batter's strike zone had he been in the box.

What is the call? What would the call be if the pitcher had stopped his motion and didn't pitch?

Rule 7: Batting

An array of rules cover batting. These rules include batting-order situations, delays by the batter, batter's interference calls and a host of other situations. Here are four such situations that you will need to know how to call. Choose how you would rule and then check your judgments against the answers beginning on page 146.

CASE 5: Batting Out of Order

Brownsburg is playing at Richmond, and Brownsburg's sixth hitter in the lineup lines a single to right field. Their eighth hitter comes to the plate next, accidentally skipping over the seventh hitter. Brownsburg's eighth hitter takes two pitches, both strikes, when the Richmond manager realizes the error and comes to the plate to tell you that the Brownsburg batter is hitting out of order. What do you call?

What is the call if the Richmond coach discovered the error after the Brownsburg batter hit a two-run homer but before a pitch was made to the next hitter? What is the call if the Brownsburg batter hit a two-run homer and the mistake wasn't discovered until after a pitch had been made to the next hitter?

CASE 6: Delaying Entry Into Batter's Box

Jamestown and Westwood are tied 5-5 going into the seventh inning. The Jamestown batter leading off the top of the seventh tries to upset Westwood's pitcher by delaying his entry into the batter's box. The pitcher, seeing that the Jamestown hitter is not in the box, doesn't assume his position on the pitcher's plate. Twenty seconds elapse. What is the call?

CASE 7: In or Out of the Batter's Box?

In a game against Pittsfield, an Independence batter assumes his batting stance with his right foot partially on the back line and partially outside the back line of the batter's box. Is this stance within the rules?

What is the call if the batter's foot was completely outside the back line of the batter's box? What is the call if the batter's foot was on the back line but no part of his foot was outside the line?

CASE 8: Batter's Interference?

York has a runner on first with one out and two strikes on the batter. On the next pitch from the Centralia pitcher, the runner takes off on an attempted steal of second. The York batter swings and misses and interferes with the Centralia catcher's attempt to throw out the York runner, who slides safely into second. What is the call?

Rule 8: Baserunning

We could fill a book with baserunning situations and rules, because, as you know, almost anything can, and does, happen on the base paths. Study the *NFHS Baseball Rules Book* well, because you'll rule on an almost endless variety of plays and situations involving base runners—everything from missed bases to overthrows to obstruction to interference to appeal plays and beyond. Here are a few examples of the baserunning plays you have to rule on. Consider how you would respond in each situation and check your judgments against the answers beginning on page 147.

CASE 9: Catcher's Obstruction

Centralia has a runner on second with one out. On the next pitch, the Jamestown catcher obstructs the Centralia batter, but the batter manages to hit a ground ball to the second baseman, who throws him out at first. The Jamestown first baseman fires over to third in an attempt to get the advancing Centralia runner, but his throw sails over the third baseman's head and the Centralia runner jogs home, scoring easily. Does the catcher's obstruction negate the run?

CASE 10: Missing a Base

Pittsfield has a runner on third with no one out against Westwood. The Pittsfield batter lifts a fly ball to short center field. As the center fielder makes the catch, the runner legally tags up and heads toward home. The runner sees that the play is going to be close and as the Westwood catcher stretches for the ball to tag the runner out, the runner attempts to hurdle the catcher's outstretched arms. The throw bounces in front of home plate and skips past the catcher into dead-ball territory.

As the Pittsfield runner attempts to hurdle the catcher, his foot hits the catcher's glove. Both the runner and the catcher tumble to the ground. The runner never touches the plate, but with the ball in dead-ball territory, he gets up and jogs back to the dugout. What is the ruling? Is the runner out for missing the plate or for attempting to hurdle the catcher? Or is he safe because the catcher didn't apply a tag and the ball is dead?

Would the ruling change if the runner had come back to touch home plate?

CASE 11: Appeal Play

Richmond has a runner on first. On the next pitch from the Brownsburg pitcher, the Richmond batter singles to right. The runner on first misses second base on his way to third but reaches third before the throw arrives from the right fielder.

The playing action is over, but the ball is still alive. The Brownsburg third baseman, who has the ball, tags the runner while the runner is standing on third base. What is the call?

Would the call be any different if the third baseman tosses the ball to the second baseman, who then steps on second base while holding the ball? What if the third baseman merely states that the runner missed second base but takes no action? What if the third baseman calls time, states that the runner missed second, but still takes no action?

CASE 12: Runner's Interference
Independence has runners on second and third against York. The batter hits a sharp grounder toward the York shortstop. As the Independence runner on second tries to advance to third, he pushes the shortstop. As a result, the runner on third scores, the runner on second makes it to third, and the batter is safe at first. What is the call?

Answers

Here you can check your answers to the cases presented in this chapter.

Case 1: Pitching After Balking
Once the Jamestown pitcher balked, the ball is dead. It doesn't matter if the batter swings and misses, if he swings and hits the ball, or if the ball goes back to the backstop. The ball is dead immediately when the balk occurs, and the balk penalty is enforced—meaning, of course, that the runner on third is awarded home.

Case 2: Warm-Up Throws
The Westwood starting pitcher who was late to the mound to begin the third inning can take five warm-up throws if he can get them in within the one-minute time limit, which begins immediately after the third out of the previous half inning. The umpire-in-chief makes the judgment about how many pitches to allow if a pitcher is late in getting to the mound, but allowing a pitcher warm-up pitches is not advisable because of the potential risk of injury to the pitcher's arm. A relief pitcher coming in gets eight throws.

Case 3: Feinting Toward Third Base
In both situations the York pitcher has committed a balk. The pitcher must step toward third base when feinting there. In the second case, with the feint toward third and the throw to first, the move would have been OK if the pitcher had first stepped toward third before throwing to first.

In an effort to avoid a batting order error, you should make sure a team is clear on batting order and cards are error-free.

Case 4: Time Not Granted to Batter

In the first situation, with the Centralia batter stepping fully out of the box without being granted time and the pitcher throwing a pitch clearly out of the strike zone, you should call a strike on the batter, no matter where the pitch was. The ball is alive, and the runner can advance at his own risk. If the pitcher doesn't throw a pitch, you should still call a strike on the batter for stepping out of the box and delaying the game.

Case 5: Batting Out of Order

Timing makes all the difference in this type of call. If the Richmond coach discovers the error with two strikes on the batter who is batting out of order, there is no penalty. The seventh batter (the one who was skipped) takes the place of the eighth batter, inheriting the two-strike count. If the Brownsburg runner on first had advanced by a steal or wild pitch while the incorrect batter was batting, the advance is legal.

But if the Richmond coach discovers the error after the Brownsburg batter clubs a home run but before a pitch is made to the next hitter, the seventh batter (the one who was skipped) is called out, the home run is negated, the runner returns to first base, and the eighth batter—the one whose home run was just canceled—bats again, with no balls or strikes.

(The same would be true if the eighth hitter had made an out and the error was discovered before a pitch was made to the next hitter. The seventh batter would be declared out, the runner would remain on first, and the eighth batter would return to the plate with no count.)

If the batting-order error was discovered after the eighth batter hit a home run and the ninth batter had a pitch delivered to him, the home run is allowed, both runs count and no correction is made. The seventh batter will bat in his proper spot in the lineup the next time around, and the ninth batter remains at the plate.

Case 6: Delaying Entry Into Batter's Box
The Jamestown batter is charged with a strike. Although the Westwood pitcher didn't deliver a pitch within the allotted 20 seconds, he can't pitch until the batter is set in the batter's box and therefore he isn't penalized.

Case 7: In or Out of the Batter's Box
The Independence batter who has his right foot partially outside the batter's box is in violation of the rules. You should instruct the batter to assume his stance so that neither foot is outside the lines of the batter's box. You should do likewise if one of his feet is entirely outside the box.

Case 8: Batter's Interference?
Because the York batter interfered with the Centralia catcher's attempt to throw out the runner trying to stealing second, the batter is out for interference. If, in your judgment, the catcher could have thrown out the York base stealer, you can call him out also. If not, the York runner must return to first.

Case 9: Catcher's Obstruction
The Centralia coach has a choice to make. He can choose to take the result of the play, meaning that the batter, who was obstructed, is out and the runner scores. Alternatively, he can take the catcher's obstruction penalty, which would result in the runner remaining on second and the batter being awarded first base.

Case 10: Missing a Base
If Westwood appeals the play, the Pittsfield runner should be called out—not for hurdling the catcher, which is legal, but for missing home plate. If the runner comes back and touches home, the run counts.

Case 11: Appeal Play
In all cases, the appeal by the Brownsburg team is legal and the runner is out.

Case 12: Runner's Interference

This is partly a judgment call that depends on what you think would have likely transpired. The part that isn't a judgment call concerns the runner on second who interfered with the shortstop fielding the ball; he is automatically out for interference. With the interference call, the ball becomes dead.

Now comes the judgment part. If, in your opinion, the shortstop could have fielded the ball and thrown out the runner trying to score, the runner on third should also be called out. If you believe that the shortstop was about to field the ball, tag the runner on second and retire the batter-runner at first as well, you should call those two runners out. If you feel that the shortstop, even in fielding the ball cleanly, could not have retired any runner, then only the runner on second is out. When interference occurs, any runners must return to the bases they occupied at the time of the interference, unless they had scored before the time of interference or were put out.

CHAPTER 11

KEEPING IT FAIR

The final two rules we'll consider are Rule 9: Scoring and Record Keeping and Rule 10: Umpiring. As with the previous chapters on rules, we'll present cases for you to make calls on, and present the answers at the end of the chapter.

Rule 9: Scoring and Record Keeping

Rule 9 covers an assortment of scoring and record-keeping situations, including failure to retouch bases, runs scoring on plays in which third outs are made, missed bases and other plays that affect scoring or recording plays. Here are a few of those cases. Consider how you would respond in each case and check your judgments against the answers beginning on page 152.

CASE 1: Two Runners Advancing Illegally

Jamestown has runners on first and second against York. The Jamestown batter hits a deep drive to center field that looks to be uncatchable, but the York center fielder makes a great catch. The runner on second tags up and is able to score all the way from second, but he misses third base on his way home. The runner on first advances to third, but without tagging up. What is the call?

CASE 2: Runner Scoring on Third Out?

Brownsburg has runners on second and third with one out when the batter lifts a long fly ball to center field that is caught by the Pittsfield center fielder. The runner on third remains in contact with his base, expecting the catch to be made, but the runner on second does not tag up and is nearly at third by the time the center fielder makes the catch.

The center fielder throws the ball to the second baseman, and the ball arrives before the runner who was on second can get back to the bag. Meanwhile, the runner on third, who had legally tagged up, advances and scores. The second baseman makes the putout at second for the third out.

What is the call if the runner on third scored before the putout was made? Is the call any different if the runner on third crossed the plate after the putout at second was made?

CASE 3: Runner Missing a Base

Richmond has a runner on first with two outs against Centralia. The Richmond batter hits an inside-the-park home run, but in circling the bases he misses second. What is the call?

Would the call be any different if the batter-runner had missed first base instead of second?

CASE 4: Runner Scoring on Force-Out?

Independence has the bases loaded with one out against Westwood. The Independence batter singles to right, scoring two runs, although you saw the runner on second miss third base as he made the turn and headed home to score. Meanwhile, the runner on first rounds second and is thrown out at third. At the end of the action, Westwood appeals the play and you declare the runner on second base out for missing third. How many runs score?

Rule 10: Umpiring

Rule 10 covers a variety of situations that could occur before, during or after a game. This rule has to do with correcting umpire errors, handling protests, an umpire's jurisdiction before a game or outside the confines of the field, and an umpire's behavior. Here are some of the cases that might come your way. Decide how you would rule and then check your answers against the answers beginning on page 153.

CASE 5: Protest Lodged

Pittsfield, losing 5-4 in the bottom of the seventh inning against York, has a runner on second with two outs. The next batter singles to center, and the runner on second rounds third and heads home, hoping to score the tying run. The York center fielder momentarily juggles the ball, allowing the runner enough time to beat the throw home. The Pittsfield runner touches the plate and then maliciously runs over the catcher, who is waiting for the late throw. As plate umpire, you eject the Pittsfield runner and nullify his run—meaning that the game is over and York has won, 5-4.

As both teams begin to go to their respective dugouts, the Pittsfield coach informs the field umpire that the run should score, because the Pittsfield runner touched the plate before the malicious contact occurred. The field umpire summons you. You disagree, prompting the coach to lodge a protest with you. Is this protest on record or not?

CASE 6: Play Suspended by Rain

Brownsburg and Jamestown are in the bottom of the third inning when rain begins to fall, and you, as plate umpire, suspend play. The rain continues for 30 minutes. Are you obliged to call the game at this point?

CASE 7: Correcting an Umpire Error

Westwood has a runner on first with one out against Centralia with a three-ball, two-strike count on the batter. On the next pitch, the runner takes off on an attempted steal, but the pitch is ball four. You, as field umpire, move into position near second base.

   Neither you, the runner nor the second baseman are aware that the pitch was ball four, and the Centralia catcher fires down to second, nabbing the base runner on the attempted steal. You immediately call the Westwood runner out, and the runner begins to trot back to his dugout. While the runner is on the base path and heading back to his dugout, the second baseman, realizing now that ball four had been called, alertly tags the runner a second time, this time figuring the runner would be out because, although he was awarded second base automatically because of the walk, he moved off the base after touching it. So he tags the runner again and holds the ball aloft for you to make the call. What do you do?

If an error is brought to your attention during a game, you should correct it immediately.

CASE 8: Changing an Incorrect Score

Richmond is hosting Independence and enters the bottom of the seventh inning trailing 8-3. Richmond rallies and scores several runs. According to the scoreboard, the score is 8-7 when, with two outs and the bases loaded, a Richmond batter strikes out, thus ending the game with an apparent final score of 8-7 in favor of Independence.

But the Richmond coach hustles over with his scorebook and contends that his team scored five runs in that inning, not four. After looking at the scorebook, you agree with the Richmond coach: Five runs had scored, although the scoreboard operator had posted only four runs on the board for that half inning.

What is the ruling? Would the ruling be any different if the coach had brought the error to your attention before the game ended?

Answers

Following are the answers to the cases presented in this chapter.

Case 1: Two Runners Advancing Illegally

Both runners are out if York appeals the plays. The runner on second would be out for failing to touch third base. The runner on first base would be out for failing to tag up after the catch.

Case 2: Runners Scoring on Third Out?

The Brownsburg runner at second is the third out of the inning. If his teammate on third scored before the third out was recorded, the run counts. If his teammate scored after the third out was made, the run does not count. The inning ended with a play in which the third out was not a force-out. No runs can score if the third out is a force-out or if the batter does not reach first.

Case 3: Runner Missing a Base

When all action stops, you should rule the Richmond batter-runner out for missing second base—if the Centralia team appeals the play. If they don't appeal, you have no call to make and all the runs score. Had the batter-runner missed first base and had Centralia appealed, no runs would score, because it's a timing play and the third out was made before the run scored.

Case 4: Runner Scoring on Force-Out?

No runs score because Westwood appealed the play, resulting in the runner originally on second base being forced out at third after he missed that base. Remember, no runs can score on a force-out if that out is the third out of the inning.

Case 5: Protest Lodged

The Pittsfield coach's protest is on record, if the state association allows protests, because he lodged the protest with you before you and your crew left the field. If you, as umpire-in-chief, had realized that the play had not been called correctly, the game would resume, as long as an umpire had remained on the field. The run should count, you should eject the Pittsfield player who scored the tying run and the game should continue.

Case 6: Play Suspended by Rain

No, you're not obliged to call the game after it has been suspended for 30 minutes by rain. You should call the game when you are convinced that field conditions have degenerated to the point where play would be difficult and hazardous. Although it's customary to wait 30 minutes before calling a game, you're not required to make that decision at the end of those 30 minutes. If, after a half-hour delay, a chance remains that the game can be resumed, withhold any announcement of calling the game until you are certain that no further play will be possible within a reasonable amount of time.

Case 7: Correcting an Umpire Error

You rectify your mistake by putting the runner back on second base as the batter-runner goes to first base. Your decision caused the Westwood runner to leave second base; when you called him out, he was simply obeying your call. Correct the call and allow the runner to remain where he would have been, had you not misled him.

Case 8: Changing an Incorrect Score

The correct ruling is that the game goes into extra innings with the score tied 8-8. Because the Richmond coach brought the error to your attention before you and your crew left the playing field, and because the scoring error has a potential effect on the outcome of the game, you correct the score and, in this case, the game goes on. If the Richmond coach had not brought the inaccuracy to your attention before you and your crew left the field, the score would have stood as posted: 8-7. If such an error is brought to your attention at any time during a game, you would rectify the score immediately.

NFHS Officiating Baseball Signals

A. Do Not Pitch

B. Play Ball

C. Time-Out, Foul Ball or Dead Ball

D. Delayed Dead Ball

E. Strike or Out

F. Infield Fly

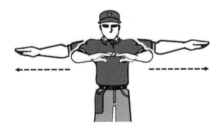

G. Safe

H. Fair Ball

I. Foul Tip

J. Count

K. Time Play

GLOSSARY

appeal play—A play in which a coach appeals a play, believing that the other team broke the rules in some way. Examples include batting out of order, requesting assistance on a batter's half swing, a runner missing a base and a runner leaving a base too soon on a tag-up play.

balk—An illegal act committed by the pitcher with a runner or runners on base. Each runner advances one base when a pitcher commits a balk.

baseline—The direct line between bases. A runner is out if he runs more than 3 feet out of the baseline to avoid being tagged or to hinder a fielder, unless the runner is trying to avoid interfering with the fielder as the fielder is attempting to field a batted ball. The base runner establishes his own baseline directly between his position and the base he is advancing to.

base umpire—An umpire assigned to a base—first, second or third.

checked swing—Occurs when a batter starts to swing and then stops. The final decision is based on whether the batter struck at the ball.

conference—A conference is charged when a coach meets with a player or players on his team. On defense, a team cannot be granted more than three conferences per seven-inning game. On offense, a team cannot have more than one charged conference per inning.

dead ball—In numerous situations, the ball becomes dead and a play is over. See Rule 5 in the *NFHS Baseball Rules Book.*

delayed dead ball—A play in which the ball becomes dead only after the umpire calls, "Time."

double first base—Two bases that are side by side at first. The white base is in fair territory and is used by the fielder; a colored base is in foul territory and is used by the batter-runner only on the initial play at first base.

fair ball—A batted ball that settles in fair ground between home and third base or between home and first base, or is on or over fair ground when bounding to the outfield past first or third base.

foul ball—A batted ball that settles in foul ground between home and third base or between home and first base, or that bounds past first or third base on or over foul territory and first touches ground in foul territory beyond first or third base.

illegal pitch—With any illegal pitch, the ball becomes dead. With no runner on base, a ball is awarded to the batter. With runners on base, a balk is called and all runners move up one base. Illegal pitches occur when, for example, the pitcher puts a foreign substance on the ball, spits on the ball or glove, or takes the pitching hand to the mouth without distinctly wiping off the hand before it touches the ball.

illegally batted ball—A ball hit while breaking a rule, such as batting with a foot touching the ground completely outside the lines of the batter's box or touching home plate. The ball is dead and the batter is out.

infield fly—A fair fly ball (not a line drive or an attempted bunt) that an infielder can catch with normal effort with less than two outs with runners on first and second or with the bases loaded. The batter is automatically out.

interference—Can occur in a number of situations when a batter or base runner interferes with the fielding of, or throwing of, the ball.

mercy rule—Some associations have a mercy rule in effect to end lopsided games earlier than normal. Check with your state association.

obstruction—Obstruction occurs in a number of instances when a fielder obstructs a base runner. Obstruction can be intentional, such as a fake tag, or unintentional, such as when the defensive player is illegally in the path of the runner. The umpire has the authority to determine what base to award to the runner.

out—A batter makes an out in numerous ways, including hitting a fair or foul ball caught by a fielder, striking out, bunting foul on the third strike, hitting a ball that is ruled an infield fly and being thrown out at first on a ground ball.

plate umpire—The umpire behind the plate, also known as the umpire-in-chief.

strike—A strike is recorded in various situations, including a swing and miss by a batter, a called strike taken by a batter, a pitch hit foul and a pitch bunted foul.

strike zone—The space over home plate with the top of the zone being halfway between the batter's shoulders and waistline and the bottom of the zone being the knees when a batter assumes his natural batting stance.

suspended game—A called game to be completed at a later date.

three-foot lane—The lane drawn over the last half of the distance to first base. The batter-runner must stay inside this lane while the ball is being fielded or thrown to first base, unless in doing so he will interfere with the fielding or throwing of the ball.

time-out (immediate dead ball)—The ball becomes dead immediately in a number of situations, including when a pitch touches the batter or his clothing (even if the batter swings at it), when a foul ball is not caught, when an umpire calls interference, when a fair batted ball touches a runner or umpire before touching any fielder and before passing any fielder other than the pitcher, and when a spectator touches a ball.

umpire-in-chief—The home-plate umpire. He or she calls and counts balls and strikes; signals fair balls; verifies out call(s); calls, "Foul ball!", except on a caught foul fly ball, while signaling a foul ball, except on fair or foul situations commonly called by the field umpire or umpires; and makes all decisions on the batter. The umpire-in-chief makes all decisions except for those commonly reserved for the field umpire or base umpires.

INDEX

Note: The italicized *f* following page numbers refers to figures.

ABOUT THE AUTHOR

Officiating Baseball was written by the American Sport Education Program (ASEP) in cooperation with the National Federation of State High School Associations (NFHS). Based in Indianapolis, the NFHS is the rules authority for high school sports in the United States. Hundreds of thousands of officials nationwide and throughout the world rely on the NFHS for officiating guidance. ASEP is a division of Human Kinetics, based in Champaign, Illinois, and has been a world leader in providing educational courses and resources to professional and volunteer coaches, officials, parents and sport administrators for more than 20 years. ASEP and the NFHS have teamed up to offer courses for high school officials through the NFHS Officials Education Program.

NFHS Officials Education Program

ONLINE EDUCATION FOR ON-THE-GO OFFICIA

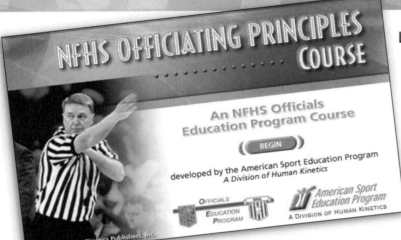

Late-night games.
Weekend tournament
Pregame preparation
Postgame reflection.

As an official, just becaus
you keep track of time
doesn't mean you have
any. So instead of taking
even more time out to
attend another officials
clinic, explore the
timesaving, schedule-friendly online cour
offered through the **NFHS Officials Education Program.**

A joint effort between the **National Federation of State High School Associations (NFH**
and the **American Sport Education Program (ASEP)**, the NFHS Officials Education Progr
features a two-part, Internet-delivered curriculum covering officiating principles and
sport-specific methods based on NFHS rules.

Available now is *NFHS Officiating Principles*, a course applicable to all officials regardle
of their sport. The course shows you how to determine your officiating philosophy
and style, improve communication, develop decision-making skills, manage conflict,
understand legal responsibilities, manage your officiating career, and much more.

Coming soon: *Officiating [Sport] Methods* courses for softball, football, soccer, basketb
wrestling, and baseball cover the sport-specific methods and mechanics of officiating a
they apply to NFHS rules and regulations. The officiating [sport] book that you have in
your hands serves as the text for the course. Check the ASEP Web site at www.ASEP.com
for updates on course availability.

NFHS Officials Education Program offers you the continuing education you need as an
official on a schedule that's right for you. Registration fees are only $75 per course and
include a course text, CD-ROM, study guide, exam, and entry into the National Officials
Registry. For more information, or to register for a course, visit **www.ASEP.com** or call
ASEP at **800-747-5698.**

2442SD
03-11-05 32572

American Sport Education Program
A DIVISION OF HUMAN KINETICS